MISSION POSSIBLE

STRATEGIES AND COMPETENCIES OF SUCCESSFUL CORPORATE TURNAROUND EXECUTIVES

MARTIN CROUS, PH.D.

Note for Librarians: A cataloguing record for this book is available from Library
and Archives Canada at www.collectionscanada.ca/amicus/index-e.html
ISBN 1-4251-1529-2

Offices in Canada, USA, Ireland and UK

Book sales for North America and international:
Trafford Publishing, 6E–2333 Government St.,
Victoria, BC V8T 4P4 CANADA
phone 250 383 6864 (toll-free 1 888 232 4444)
fax 250 383 6804; email to orders@trafford.com
Book sales in Europe:
Trafford Publishing (UK) Limited, 9 Park End Street, 2nd Floor
Oxford, UK OX1 1HH UNITED KINGDOM
phone +44 (0)1865 722 113 (local rate 0845 230 9601)
facsimile +44 (0)1865 722 868; info.uk@trafford.com
Order online at:
trafford.com/06-3286

10 9 8 7 6 5 4 3 2

ACKNOWLEDGMENT

This book has been in the making for several years, and through that time I've had support from all my friends and family. To all of you that made this possible, thank you.

ABOUT THE AUTHOR

With over 20 years of business development and sales and marketing expertise, Dr. Crous has developed strong communication, negotiation and presentation skills focused on turnarounds and start ups, international business development, training, development, mentoring and coaching, corporate strategy, sales and sales management, marketing, brand diagnostics and strategic planning, motivating sales and marketing professionals, and market research and competitor intelligence.

His travels have taken him all over the world, and he has done work in business development in both hemispheres. His education includes an international Ph.D. and an M.B.A. in business focusing on corporate strategy.

Please visit: www.martincrous.com

INTRODUCTION

Mission Possible is a story of a general overview and the results of research done on the turnaround or recovery of corporate organizations. These strategies can be used and implemented by any organization, small or large.

I chose to write a "semi-novel" to make the results of my team's research more understandable and easier to read. The results of this research are not fiction, however; this work was done in the real world of business by real professionals. If we understand and apply some of these results and principles in our present or future business organizations, then we can and will be successful.

Most businesses experience a crisis at some stage during their growth from their small entrepreneurial beginnings to their mature years as large organizations. These crises are crossroads where some companies will succeed in their recoveries, whereas others will not recover.

This book will answer two common questions.

1. Does corporate recovery or turnaround require strategies and management processes that are different from those applied to stable organizations?
2. Does the chief executive officer that effects such a recovery need specific competencies and characteristics in order to be successful?

As indicated in this book, the research given here aims to establish the relationships that exist between the:

1. Competencies and personalities of the executives of successfully recovered organizations
2. Their choices of recovery strategies,
3. Their structuring of key organizational processes and the financial success of the business organizations they manage.

Two groups of business organizations were selected based on four criteria:

1. Profit growth
2. Revenue growth
3. Return on sales
4. Return on assets.

Four organizations that have been successfully recovered were then compared in terms of the above variables to four organizations with declining financial performance.

The results of this research indicate that in terms of *intervention strategies*, the business organizations that have been successfully recovered differed significantly in comparison to those in decline in their choice of intervention strategies, the activities they engage in, and the issues on which they spend their time.

The results of this research also indicate that, in terms of *the nature and structure of key management and organizational processes,* the business organizations that have been successfully recovered, in comparison to those organizations in decline, differed significantly in their structuring.

The results of this research further indicate that the chief executive officers (CEOs) of the business organizations that have been successfully recovered differed from the CEOs of other organizations in terms of *personality, managerial competence,* and *cognitive capacity.*

There is sufficient evidence, therefore, to suggest that

1. Certain elements of a corporate recovery strategy were more successful than others
2. Successfully recovered organizations structured key organizational processes differently
3. The CEOs of recovered organizations possess distinct personality characteristics, behavioral competencies, and cognitive capacities.

Good luck in your search for these principles and for your own understanding of *Mission Possible.*

chapter 1

IT IS A BEAUTIFUL Monday morning as I drive to work. Not a cloud in the sky. "Quite unusual for this time of year," I hear the weatherman on the car radio proclaim. My consulting company is in a rut. We have been doing the same sort of consulting to businesses for the past ten years, focusing on business development in the area of developing our customers' sales and marketing efforts. Finally arriving at work, after a full hour's morning commute, I park my BMW in my assigned parking space. As I walk toward the front door of the building, I am thinking ahead to our usual Monday morning executive meeting.

"Good morning, Adam," Linda, my office manager, greets me as I enter.

"Morning, Linda," I reply automatically as I continue walking toward my office. Today is the day that things have to change. We need to find a way to add more value to our business and in such a way that will help our customers do the same.

After setting my briefcase in my office, I enter our conference room, or "mission control," as my team has affectionately named it, at 8 a.m., sharp. "Good morning all," I greet them with enthusiasm.

"Good morning," come their simultaneous replies. Three of the team members are seated nicely around the table. As usual, John is late. I look at the team. Scott, who was a freight manager for more than eight years, has worked on our transport accounts for the past three years. Carin, who was in the pharmaceutical and medical device industry as national sales manager for over nine years, has been working on our medical accounts for the past five years. Tim, who was a national manager for a major retail company for fourteen years, has been responsible for our retail accounts the past six years. John was the CEO of a chemical company for five years and has been working on our chemical industry accounts for the past seven years.

Just as I am about to sit down, John rushes into mission control. "Sorry I'm late," he mumbles as he takes a seat next to Scott.

"All I could think about this weekend," I begin, "was that we need to take our company into another stage in our business life cycle. We have enough responsible people in our office to continue managing the projects we're busy with right now. I suggest that we, as the executive team, need to find another way that we can (a) add value to our company and (b) add another product offering for our present and future customers."

"In the transport industry," Scott says, "there has always been a stage where companies have had crises. Maybe we can offer solutions to such problems."

"I've seen the same problems in my industry," John says.

"Me, too," says Carin, and Tim also nods his head in agreement.

"These are exciting observations," I say, and we begin to discuss possibilities and come to the conclusion that at some stage during their growth phase from their small entrepreneurial beginnings to their mature years as large organizations, most businesses experience crises. These crises, we believe, are crossroads where some will succeed in recovering their vitality and grow to greater heights, while others will dwindle into a spiral of degeneration.

"So it will be our mission," I say as our discussion comes to its logical conclusion, "to find out if the executives of recovered companies, or turnaround organizations, require specific strategies and management processes that are different from the executives of stable organizations. We also need to find out if the chief executive officer who effects such a recovery needs specific competencies and characteristics in order to be successful."

I can feel the excitement, enthusiasm, and energy in the room. The team has decided to focus on a new direction.

I stand at the white board, marker in hand. "So our mission will be," I say, writing as I speak, "to establish the relationships that exist between the:

1. Competencies and personalities of successful corporate recovery executives
2. Their choice of recovery strategies

3. Their structuring of key organizational processes and the financial success of the business organizations they manage.

I turn back to them. "Team, it's 1:15. Let's take a two-hour lunch break and at the same time see to it that we delegate our present projects and responsibilities to other team members in our office." As they stand up to leave the room, I remember something else. "Oh, yes. I almost forgot. Please bring something to make notes on this afternoon."

One by one we leave mission control.

✻ ✻ ✻

It is three o'clock when we file back into mission control and take our seats. I begin the afternoon's work.

"We need to do some research on this topic," I say. "I thought about this during lunch. It's going to be a long, slow process. We will select two groups of business organizations based on four criteria—*profit growth, revenue growth, return on sales*, and *return on assets*. We need to investigate a group of organizations that have been successfully recovered and compare them with organizations with declining financial performance in terms of the variables mentioned.

"We expect," I continue, "that the results of our research will indicate that, in terms of *intervention strategies*, the business organizations that have been successfully recovered, in comparison to those in decline, differ significantly in their choice of intervention strategies, the activities they engage in, and the issues on which they spend their time. Let us also assume that the results of our research will further indicate that, in terms of *the nature and structure of key management and organizational processes,* the organizations that have been successfully recovered will differ significantly from those in decline in their structuring. Let us further assume that the results of our research will further indicate that the CEOs of the organizations that have been successfully recovered differ from the CEOs of other organizations in terms of *personality, managerial competence,* and *cognitive capacity.*

"It is," I conclude, "our expectation also that there will be sufficient evidence to suggest that certain elements of a corporate recovery strategy will be more successful than others, that successfully recovered organizations structure key organizational processes differently, and that the CEOs of recovered organizations possess distinct personality characteristics, behavioral competencies, and cognitive capacities."

We now discuss the mission of this project and what the outcome will mean for us as a company. Carin, as always, brings us back to ordinary life.

"It's 6:40," she says, "and I need to get home to my family."

We all agree to get back together the next day at 9 a.m. to continue exploring our new-found mission.

chapter 2

I ENTER MISSION CONTROL at 8:45 the next morning and am pleasantly surprised to see that everyone is already present and reading business books.

Tim, who completed his MBA at Harvard Business School, looks up and says, "After our meeting yesterday, I got together all the books I could find about the role of modern business organizations, change and turbulence in corporate organizations, the need for research into corporate recovery, and the size of corporate decline problems."

"Thank you, Tim," I say. "This will be a good start for us. We need to read as much as we can about what our new mission is all about. We'll need to get together for the next few mornings to compare our research and notes. I'll give you all a week for your research. Let's convene again on Monday morning."

❋ ❋ ❋

"Morning, Adam" Linda greets me on the next Monday morning.

After my usual automatic salutation I stroll into mission control. Today my team will report back on their research in the literature.

John is excited to start. "I enjoy reading business books," he says, "and I also enjoy implementing their strategies into my business." He opens the binder he has already filled with notes.

"When Karl Marx started work on his book, *Das Kapital,* in the 1850s, the phenomenon of management was unknown," he begins. "The concept of a business enterprise was also new. The largest manufacturing company at that time was a cotton mill in Manchester, England, that employed fewer than 300 people. It was owned by Marx's collaborator, Frederick Engels. In this mill there were no managers, just charge hands, who were fellow workers.

"Rarely in human history has any institution emerged as quickly as management. Or had as great an impact so quickly," John continues. "In less than 150 years, management has transformed the social and economic fabric of the world's developed countries. It has created a global economy and set new rules for countries that would participate in that economy as equals.

"At the commencement of World War I, a few thinkers were just becoming aware of the existence of management, although at that time only a very small number of people had anything to do with business. Today, however, managers are the largest single group in the labor force of the USA.

According to the U.S. Bureau of Census, more than one third of the total labor force is classified as managerial and professional. The emergence of management also explains why for the first time in human history organizations can employ large numbers of people in productive work. No society before could support more than a handful of people. No one knew how to put people with different skills and knowledge together to achieve a common aim. The business organization has become one of the most important institutions in our social and economic system. The health and survival, or decline and death, of the business organization are critical to the social fabric of society."

"Thank you for the history lesson," Tim interjects with a smile.

But John ignores Tim and continues. "Some writers contended that management creativity, although seldom as stunning as the great achievements of the arts and sciences, led to significant management innovations in this century, notably scientific management thought, operations research, job enrichment, quality circles, brainstorming, human relations, organizational development, portfolio management, long-range planning, matrix networks and cluster structures, cost-benefit analysis, social marketing, formal managerial training, virtual organizations, and strengths, weaknesses, opportunities, threats (SWOT) analysis."

He smiles as the other members of the team nod their heads. "These innovations have had a profound influence on the shaping of our civilization and the fabric of our society," he says. "Very little else influences so profoundly the way we live and the structure of society as the way work is organized. Such innovations have had as profound an influence on human existence as relativity theory, quantum physics, psychoanalysis, cognition economics, or cubism. In most business organizations there are also numerous but less glamorous organization-specific innovations which, although not very original, are used ingeniously on a daily basis to solve problems." John closes his binder.

"Well," Carin says, also smiling, "as Tim stated, that's a lot of history." Now it's her turn to open her binder. "My report is less about history and more about facts," she tells us. "My readings were on the elements of change and turbulence within organizations and what organizations face today. Change and turbulence are phenomena of globalization, the development of transnational economies, the fuel crisis, inflation and higher interest rates, increased competition and a glut of production capacity, and privatization and deregulation."

"These issues," she says, "necessitate greater attention to management, commercial awareness, and concern for quality. Managers face complex and challenging pressures and opportunities where they must ensure the efficient use of resources while at the same time guaranteeing the long-term effectiveness of the organization.

"Despite the fact that today's business managers are better educated, better informed, and harder working than their predecessors of the 1970s and 1980s, the intensified competition and turbulence tend to make them look *less* capable. Past practices and traditional business education prepared them, like generals, to fight the *last* war not the present one, much less the *next* one."

The men around the table nod their heads, and she continues. "The emergence of turnaround management from 1948 to 1973 resulted in the growth in GNP in the

USA with an average of 3.7 percent. Unemployment was low, the inflation rate was below 5 percent, and interest rates were thus also low. American business served the growing domestic market and also expanded into Europe, Asia, and Latin America. America was a net exporter, developing a surplus at one stage of $157 billion.

"A body of business practice and literature developed which suited this environment. Vertical organizations with tall structures, narrow spans of control, and powerful staff functions suited this stable business environment. Decisions took a long time to make, given the channels one had to go through. Long-term planning became a fetish, managers were rarely fired, debt was used liberally, and management made massive concessions to unions in pay rates and work rules. Turnaround management was seldom necessary, and thus rare, in such a business climate.

"The turbulence in the business world began during the early 1970s, when environmental change accelerated and competition intensified. Oil prices sky rocketed. Prime interest rates reached 20 percent in 1981 and then fell to 8 percent in 1986. Real growth in GNP averaged only 2.3 percent from 1973 to 1985. By 1985, the U.S. net export deficit was $79 billion, down from the previous surplus of $157 billion. The Pacific Rim countries invaded U.S. overseas markets. The rate of technological change accelerated, and suddenly new items started replacing previously unassailable products." Carin looks around the table and closes her binder.

"More history," says Tim.

"Tim," I say, "I think it is important for us to see where it all started."

"Let's look at the size of corporate decline problem," he

replies. "Through the growth phase of any organization, from its small beginning to its mature years as a large organization, most organizations experience a crisis of some sort at various stages. Most organizations are likely to face financial crises at some point during their lifetime. They would be in need of a turnaround. Such organizations," he tells us, "include firms that never rise above a low performance level, firms that have swiftly risen and then collapsed, and even fashionable superstars, as well as mature, professionally managed companies with a declining trend in earnings and market share that are operating well below or near the break-even point. Such businesses face an irreversible set of decisions. Corporate collapse can follow years of outstanding success, but spectacular business failures suddenly hit the headlines.

He knows he has our full attention now. "At any point, about 15 to 20 percent of the 850 largest British manufacturers risk insolvency," he continues. "Such companies needing turnaround have in the past included some of the best names, such as Leyland and ICI. Only 24 percent of businesses in financial crisis were recovered. The majority of businesses in crisis either became insolvent or were acquired by larger competitors.

"The average age of companies from inception to bankruptcy in the UK is 5 to 7 years. In the USA, it is also 5 to 7 years, in Israel 9 to 13 years, and in Japan 31 years. The failure rate as a percentage for these countries was UK, 1-2 percent; USA, 0.5-0.7 percent; Israel, 0.2-0.7 percent; and Japan, 0.5 percent. It should be remembered, however, that the criterion for failure was actual bankruptcy. Many companies, particularly smaller ones, simply cease to exist or are acquired by larger concerns. Bankruptcy statistics therefore give a distorted view," Tim concludes, "in that they minimize the problem."

"Boring, boring, boring," John and Carin say together, getting back at Tim for his earlier remarks about history.

Ignoring this little rivalry between the senior members of the team, Scott now begins his report. "The need for research into corporate recovery," he says, standing up and walking to the front of the room, "is that during the last decade the organizational sciences have attempted to identify the key factors that determine organizational performance. Initial findings indicated that the sound application of certain principles of management (span of control, division of labor, etc.) determine organizational success. This school of thought resulted in a preoccupation with management style." We all smile as he names the popular theories: theory X, theory Y, participative management, situational leadership, contingency theories, etc. "These were the buzzwords of the end of the twentieth century," he says. "Other issues were downsizing and rightsizing, which is the belief that if the organizational design is in line with its operating requirements, efficiency will result. More recently, additional attempts are being made to isolate certain characteristics of successful organizations.

"The changing world economic environment and the resultant turbulence in all markets brought to the surface the issue of corporate recovery and turnaround management. Turnarounds are no longer special cases. They have become a familiar part of business life. The literature on turnarounds is of fairly recent origin. The serious study of corporate failure and collapse only began in the 1970s. Until the early eighties very little had been written and published on business strategies applied in turning around business organizations in crisis. The growth of turnaround management to its current prominent status has largely been due to narrower profit margins, to a less forgiving attitude toward poor quality and service, and to shareholders and investors putting pressure on the management teams of companies to become more effective and profitable.

"The turnaround phase," he is coming to his conclusion now, "is an abnormal period in the history of the organization. It often requires approaches that are quite different from approaches that are appropriate for entrepreneurial or stable companies. We might conclude that the revival of a business from sickness is one of the most crucial events in a society where the survival of a company is intertwined with the fortunes or tragedies of all the men, women, and children who are dependent on its success for their livelihood. The fabric of the microsociety surrounding even one organization is dependent on and at the mercy of the execution of a successful turnaround." Scott gives us a brief, ironic bow and takes his seat at the table.

Just then Linda arrives with lunch.

"Good grief," I say, looking at my wristwatch, "is that the time already?" It is noon.

We all eagerly approach Linda's catered lunch. "Thanks, Linda," Scott says. "This is just what the doctor ordered." He is trying to look as handsome as he can and looking at Linda as if she is the only person in the room. Linda replies with a pretty smile.

After we have all eaten heartily, we're ready to resume today's informal seminar on management theory.

"Now that you've all reported on your findings," I tell them, "it's my turn to give feedback on what I've found and also on the reason for this research." I can see that they're all ready to take notes.

"It is possible to predict corporate crisis and failure," I begin. "Failure can be averted when management changes its approach, reappraises its strategy, and takes determined steps to prevent failure. Corporate recovery requires management strategies that are different from those applied to stable organizations. Not only are strategies for revival different, but priorities are also changing dramatically. The nature of a recovery situation is vastly different from the nature of a stable and profitable situation.

"Corporate recovery, or turnaround, is about the management of business organizations that are in crisis and will become insolvent unless specific actions are taken to restore their profitability. One way of approaching the phenomenon of corporate recovery is to state that it can be reduced to the improvement of profitability. Profitability can further be reduced to decreasing cost and/or increasing revenues. Decreasing costs involves reducing costs or increasing productivity. Increasing revenue, on the other hand, involves improving pricing and marketing and better product mixing.

"These are the essentials of turnaround management. They can be achieved by changing management, restructuring, divestiture, professionalizing systems, and a host of other managerial behaviors. It is the purpose of this mission of ours to establish whether a relationship exists between (a) the behavioral competencies, personalities, and managerial styles of successful corporate recovery executives and their structuring of managerial processes and intervention strategies, and (b) the financial success of the business organizations they manage. These relationships must be described in terms of the conditions under which they occur and the extent to which they lead to successful recovery.

"For the purpose of our new mission, our team must decide that the premise that decline might be largely caused internally is due to the fact that management has mismanaged or failed to react to human and organizational crisis.

I now begin the PowerPoint presentation that I prepared last night. "Questions that need to be answered will be as follows," I tell the team.

1. Does corporate decline suggest then that management in general, but the CEO in particular, followed managerial strategies that were inadequate to deal with the situation?

2. Does it also suggest that management in general, but the CEO in particular, did not structure organizational processes effectively?

3. Does it suggest that the managerial competencies, cognitive capacity and personality characteristics of management in general, but the CEO in particular, have a co-producer relationship with the crisis situation?

I look at the team. "Let us make these questions our research questions," I suggest. "The rationale behind our research comes from us, the team. It will be argued and evidence will be mustered to the effect that corporate decline, and subsequent successful recovery, is highly dependent on –" I raise a finger for each point " – (a) the competencies of the CEO, (b) the intervention strategies chosen, and (c) the structuring of key organizational and managerial processes."

The team members look up from their notes.

"How fast the day has gone!" I exclaim as I look at the clock. "Let's meet again next Monday and use the week to do some more literature research on corporate collapse, recovery, definition, symptoms, causes, co-producers, and stages of corporate decline. We will also need to look at recovery interventions, types of turnaround, and phases of turnaround."

We gather up our notes and binders and begin to walk out of mission control.

"All the best with your literature research." I tell them.

chapter 3

IT IS ANOTHER MONDAY morning, two weeks after we started this new mission. Today we are evaluating more of the literature research.

"Carin," I begin, "will you please make notes on the large writing pad on the tripod. Scott, will you pin the pages to the walls of mission control. Then we'll have adequate records of our research."

Carin stands up. "I suppose," she grumbles, "the only reason I have to do this is because I'm the only woman in the group!"

"And I get to do this because I'm the youngest," Scott mutters.

Ignoring them, I say, "I suggest we discuss this portion of our research as a group."

"Good idea," says Tim.

John starts. "OK, this is what I found. I noticed that there were two fields of study of turnaround management and approaches. The first incorporates researchers who study specific turnaround cases. They delve into the kinds of management actions that were used to recover a company from financial crisis. These studies provide rich insights into what management actually did and their motives for doing what they did."

We all nod as he turns a page in his notebook and continues. "The second approach includes researchers gathering and analyzing quantifiable data, such as advertising expenditure, sales from core and new products, and development costs as a percentage of total cost. And so on. The advantage of this second approach is the *objectivity* of the data, whereas the advantage of the first approach is the *richness* of the data.

"The empirical research on corporate turnaround can be classified into three categories." He pauses and turns to Carin. "This is where you can start writing," he tells her. Following his dictation, she writes the following points on the large writing pad.

1. Studies of management *strategies* leading to turnaround
2. Studies of the organizational *process* in response to crisis
3. Studies of the *economic attributes* of turnaround firms.

"The various approaches to the research of corporate recovery and turnaround," John continues, "are classified as to the method of investigation, which incorporates indirect sourcing through financial press and statistical data banks, as well as direct, first-hand study through interviews with the executives in the old, familiar case-study method. The case study consists of primary (qualitative) data, which includes recovery strategies as well as management actions, and secondary (quantitative) data, which includes the company's financial economic and market characteristics. This classification was derived from a review of the research methodologies followed in the major studies in this field.

"A classification of seventeen major studies according to the method of investigation of the approaches to the study of corporate recovery and turnaround was also made. The result of these studies was that ten organizations used the direct method of sourcing and seven the indirect. Fourteen of them used the primary source of data and three the secondary source of data."

"Let me mention," I interrupt, "that the *performance-conduct* framework as a theoretical model for the study of corporate recovery was introduced. This framework maintains that *performance* is a function of the conduct or actions of a business in areas such as pricing policies, product line and advertising strategies, research and development commitments, and so forth. *Conduct* is a function of the structure of the firm and the markets in which it operates. *Structural characteristics* include issues such as the size of the company, number of competitors, barriers to entry to the markets, and amount of product line diversification. These structural characteristics can shape the relationship of the company to other players in the market, its suppliers and buyers.

"These structural characteristics allowed some companies to be in a better position to implement successful recovery strategies," I continue as my colleagues take notes. "This was an indirect study using quantitative secondary data. As an example of indirect sourcing methods in the study of primary data, 65 turnaround cases across the world were reviewed. The review focused on the management actions taken to turn the corporations around, using as sources business publications, press releases, and reports on what actually happened. In this way, 27 turnaround elements were isolated.

"From the studies of the corporate recovery and turnaround, it seems that the qualitative case-study method (direct sourcing of primary data) seems to be the preferred method in the study of corporate recovery. It attempts to determine the psychological architecture of the company or the particular management context that led to recovery. However, in isolating the management actions that led to recovery, most of these case studies used indirect sources, such as the financial press, rather than direct sourcing of first-hand accounts given by the executive's teams of these companies."

"I understand all of this," Tim says, "but before we go on, we will need to know what the definitions of *corporate decline and recovery* are."

John turns a page of his notes. "I just read that corporate decline can be measured in various ways," he says. "The most common yardstick is declining profitability."

"Agreement has yet to be reached on what constitutes corporate decline," Carin adds, "or on the definition of a business in profit trouble. The relative view holds that decline is a situation where the key financial indices are in decline. There's a lower rate of return on sales and assets relative to past performance or relative to industry and economic trends. The absolute view holds that a decline situation is where the business is actually in the red and in a not growing situation."

She turns to another section of her binder and refers to her notes. "Three different views on the definition of corporate decline seem to emerge from a review of the major studies. The first view incorporates generalized statements of corporate decline, such as statements that a crisis is a situation where the company will become insolvent if no steps are taken to recover it. The second view of corporate decline is from a market share perspective—that a business is in financial crisis when there is a decline in sales and a resultant loss in market share. The third, and by far the most popular, notion is the view of corporate decline as a crisis of profitability and income.

"A decline situation can be defined," she continues, "as one where real profit before tax measured at constant prices has declined for three or more consecutive years, culminating in a loss situation and a cash crisis. Another definition of decline is that a firm in decline need not yet be experiencing a cash crisis. This definition can also include businesses that are not seeing any losses but are stagnant, with under-utilized assets and ineffective management. Stagnant companies can survive in this state for a number of years, but a crisis situation will eventually develop if they don't take steps to adapt.

"Profitability alone," she concludes, "is not a sufficient measure of the existence of a crisis. A very profitable firm that has grown too fast may also be in crisis due to a cash-flow problem. Reporting a loss in one single year does not necessarily indicate a case requiring turnaround."

John now continues reporting on the results of his study. "This said in the prediction of failure and success, now we need to look beyond the figures in annual reports at the management of the business. A system for assessing the viability of a company based on the causes of decline was developed. Of the seventeen factors given in this system, only two have to do with financial ratios and indices. The other fifteen relate to management and business issues. A business organization could be a failure from a managerial point of view before it is declared an economic failure and long before it is declared a legal failure."

"In the light of these various views," I remark, "and for the purpose of our research, *corporate decline* will be viewed *as a declining or deteriorating performance on a basket of indicators*. These include growth in turnover (to indicate revenue trend and market share position), profit growth from year to year (to indicate profitability trends), return on sales (net profit as a percentage of revenue to indicate internal efficiency and productivity) and return on assets (to indicate asset efficiency). This definition can include negative returns on sales; in other words, a loss situation or cash crisis."

"So," says Tim, "there is no absolute definition when looking at recovery and in most cases a recovery is defined as the opposite trend in the indices that define decline."

Everyone nods in agreement.

"Has anyone read about what the symptoms of corporate decline are?" Carin asks.

Scott raises his hand. "I read that it is often difficult to differentiate between the symptoms of corporate decline and their cause. Symptoms are typically issues that are more easily observable, even by outsiders, and entail more than just financial predictors. In traditional non-systems thinking, on the other hand, causes describe the events that lead to the manifestation of the symptoms. The symptoms of corporate decline should thus be considered along with the definition of decline because the criteria according to which decline is defined are often based on the symptoms."

He pulls a page out of his binder and nods to Carin, who returns to the large note pad, marker in hand. "Some of the symptoms of decline we found were the following." As he reads, she writes the list on a sheet of paper.

1. Decreasing profitability
2. Decreasing sales volumes at constant prices
3. Increase in debt
4. Decrease in liquidity
5. Restricted dividend policy
6. Unacceptable accounting practices
7. Top management fear
8. Management turnover
9. Declining market share
10. No planning or strategic thinking.

Carin is furiously writing and we all wait patiently for her to catch up.

Tim now stands up and says, "Another *eleven symptoms of decline* were also identified. While few businesses will exhibit all eleven, many unfortunately go unnoticed. This is because when looked at in isolation, they do not seem to be spectacular." With a nod to Carin, he reads them off and she writes them on the next sheet of paper on the large pad.

1. The company is losing money from an operating profit point of view.
2. Market share has declined steadily over a 12 to 24-month period.
3. High quality managers are departing from the firm with a degree of regularity.

4. Company pride is greatly diminished and individual initiative is at a low level. There are no new ideas.
5. The company facilities appear to be run down.
6. The company has hard time generating cash.
7. On-hand inventory exceeds the normal three-to-four-month supply level and does not reflect the mix of the product line at retail level.
8. Expense reductions have resulted in a market decrease in research and development, new product development, and advertising and promotional expenditure.
9. In case of a consumer product, the item is no longer a "brand of choice."
10. New products or items appear to be cannibalizing existing items from both a retailer and consumer purchase point of view.
11. Manufacturing facilities are operating at less than 60 percent of capacity."

As Carin is getting all this down, Scott is running around mission control posting the large sheets of paper.

Still holding two or three sheets, he turns around and says, "Others seem to agree on a number of the symptoms, notably decreasing profitability, declining market-share, management turnover, and decreasing liquidity."

After giving him time to finish posting the notes, I say, "Let's discuss the causes of corporate decline. Why do business organizations find themselves in a crisis?"

"I think," Tim replies, "we should discuss the co-producers of corporate decline described in the literature we've read, then analyze them. It's difficult to develop a clear system according to which the 'causes' of corporate decline can be categorized. This is because they are, in most cases, interrelated co-producers of the state of corporate crisis. There are internal and external causes of corporate decline. However, the feeling is that internal factors are much stronger co-producers of corporate crisis than the external factors."

He looks down at his notebook, finds the proper page, and continues. "It was found that an average of just over four factors was responsible for the decline in the cases studied, of which some were external factors and some internal factors. Of the ten most frequently reported causes of decline in the cases studied, eight relate to internal causes, while only two relate to external causes. Based on the cases of decline and recovery studied, corporate failure comes from bad management and not from external causes. While some companies struggle and others indeed fail, there are always organizations that prosper despite declining markets and adverse economic conditions. This is because their management teams know how to manage under those circumstances."

Now John speaks up again. "I learned that the seeds of future financial crisis are sown by the failure to cope with current people and organizational problems." He pauses as everyone gives this notion some thought. "The seeds of failure are internal and locked into the historical developments as the organization moves through the natural life cycles of a business," he continues. "Seventy percent of the time, the causes of decline are internal, although in some cases they're triggered by external factors. Only in approximately ten percent of the cases is decline only external.

"In claiming that there are internal and external causes

of profit problems," he continues, looking at another page of his notes, "these problems are often created through the conception and implementation of flawed strategies and tactics. These could include:

1. Adopting aggressive market-share gaining strategies
2. Ambitious mechanization and automation programs
3. Product innovation consuming a lot of capital in research and development programs
4. Penetrating new markets for which the management team has little experience or expertise
5. Frequent changes in strategic direction.

"These managers treat strategies as things that can be turned on and off at will," he adds. "They may be driving for short-term earnings at one point, but then at a later date they try to regain the market share they lost as a result of their fixation with short-term profits."

Motioning to Carin to start writing again, he continues. "The external causes identified include:

1. Increased competitive pressure
2. Recession or decrease in demand
3. Adverse price movements
4. Industrial relations policy
5. Changes in government policy
6. Excess capacity in the industry
7. Political interference and constraints
8. Hostile behavior of financial institutions
9. Poor law and order

10. Infrastructure problems.

The internal causes identified included:

1. Deficient general and functional management
2. Bad technological, location, and/or strategic choices
3. Internal conflict and politics
4. Poor work ethic
5. Corrupt management
6. Growth mania
7. Excessive conservatism
8. Bureaucratic management
9. Excessive authoritarianism
10. Poor control or coordination
11. Bad industrial relations management
12. Under-capitalization.

As the team is looking at this new list, I look up at the clock on the wall and notice that it is 4:25 p.m. "This has been another long day for all of us," I say with a yawn. "Let's continue with the literature research evaluation tomorrow morning."

chapter 4

TUESDAY MORNING ARRIVES, but Scott and Carin are not present in mission control. "The two of them have some problems to sort out in their divisions," John explains, and twenty minutes later they both arrive.

"OK," I say, motioning them all to sit down, "time to start." I look at my notes. "After reviewing what we discussed yesterday, I have decided to start with a question leading into the co-producers of decline. What or who is responsible for corporate decline? That's the question we need to address."

John, always the one who likes to talk first, begins. "My finding was that the ability of the management team, expressed as their competence to run the business, had a distinct impact on the health of the organization and also that incompetent management was undoubtedly the principal co-producer of corporate decline. Organizational and people crises were decisive in testing the capabilities of a management team and determining decline or survival."

He turns a page. "Declining companies do not cope with the internal challenges created by change. The reason for this is that businesses learn the dimensions and character of financial crisis in an organization largely because these problems are reducible to familiar, finite terms. But understanding the non-financial situation is more difficult because it is seldom finite and often a matter of subjective judgement.

"In reference to incompetent management, the sequence of decline is as follows. Top management responds to a crisis by setting up short-term control pressures that bring about ad hoc changes to the organizational structure. This change undermines the development of a clear strategy. Top management finds it difficult to face the underlying issues of strategy and performance and wherever possible avoid issues of unacceptable performance. The real fundamentals of the business are thus avoided, usually because people feel the need to protect the feelings of certain senior managers. Now the culture becomes more autocratic, more centralized, and more functional and risk-averse. As things deteriorate, the more capable managers, who are aware of the problems but frustrated in their attempts to address them, move to greener pastures. This results in a further impetus to decline. Finally, the business has been drained of any resourcefulness. It is left with managers on board who may even be the reason for the decline in the first place."

Every member of the team has seen incompetent management. Tim continues the sad tale. "The topic of incompetent management can include such issues as inadequate skill (managerial competence), management change problems, and lack of integration, lack of performance management, bad strategic choices, bureaucratic management and narrow vision."

"Another co-producer," Scott interrupts, "is the lack of managerial skill and competence. When all business factors are positive and there is no turbulence in the markets or economy, companies can continue to do well despite incompetence. When the external and internal environments become turbulent, however, incompetence shows up quickly. The personal characteristics and inadequate management skills of the CEO and his key executives play a major role in co-producing decline. Incompetence is a lack of expertise to operate the business and assimilate its growth. Incompetent or weak management can also be seen in the inability to cope and/or the inability to manage new technology or staff. Incompetent management can also appear as a lack of professionalism in...." Scott pauses momentarily as he picks up his notes. "Carin, will you please write what I am going to say now?"

Carin dutifully rises from her chair, marker in the one hand and the other hand on her waist as she waits for Scott to find his place and continue.

1. Marketing management: inappropriate pricing, wrong marketing strategy and practices and a poor product mix
2. Operations management: poor planning of operations, poor plant maintenance, poor renovation, poor inventory control, poor quality control, low productivity, and poor purchasing
3. Personnel and industrial relations management.

"Non-participative boards of directors," he continues, "do not co-produce decline. But they can prevent it by taking an active role in the design of corporate strategy and sanctioning key strategic decisions.

"I also found management change problems to be another co-producer," he adds. "An incompetent top executive team is often the result of management change decisions that were not well handled and that management change problems contributed to a situation of bad management, and corporate decline."

"Incompetent management teams," I interject, "are often the result of poor quality internal promotions. This is often the case where there is a reluctance to recruit from outside the organization, when current incumbents at lower levels in the organization, who may not yet be ready, are promoted to senior positions."

Scott continues. "Some of these managers move through the hierarchy so quickly that they don't have to live with their mistakes. They're promoted or transferred before they have to face their mistakes and also never learn the interpersonal skills they need. As a result, they find it difficult to face up to troublesome issues and deal with them inadequately and in a volatile, emotional manner." Everyone around the table nods and smiles. "Furthermore, there is a tendency to promote managers who needed little training and who will obey orders." More nods and smiles.

"Then we have the lack of integration." Carin interrupts Scott. "During organizational crisis, little understanding or trust exists between the various functions of the organization. As a result, cooperation and coordination are usually poor because senior managers lack the credibility and skills needed to build trust." She glances at Scott.

"Please do continue" he replies when he notices that she seems to be expecting some sort of sarcastic comment on her interruption.

She continues. "I also found research on the lack of performance management. This refers to lack of operating controls and a weak financial function being associated with corporate decline. Although much is said about lack of financial discipline, the reference here is to management's lack of focus on the management of performance in all its forms, from financial through to the performance of plant, equipment and people."

Now it's Tim's turn to interrupt. "Give me a chance here," he says. "What about bad strategic choices? Bad strategic choices have been identified by a number of researchers as co-producers of corporate crisis and decline. Several forms deserve attention. Carin, can you write these down, please?"

1. Over-expansion. Some researchers believed this to be the number one mistake of bad management. It can include over-diversification and sales mania. The reason why over-expansion is a problem is that in 70 percent of the cases studied, the expansion exceeded management resources.
2. Excessive leverage. This happens when a company expands at a faster rate than the internally generated cash flow can support.
3. Insufficient or excessive costly inputs. Insufficient resourcing, as well as the opposite, overresourcing, often results in a high cost structure that is associated with decline.

4. Bad technological and related choices. These are issues such as wrong technology, wrong plant scale, excess capacity, and wrong location.
5. Ill-advised growth. Mistaken diversification or expansion, poor acquisitions, and the inability to manage these.

As fast as Carin can write, Scott posts these notes on the already filled-up walls of mission control.

"Then we find bureaucratic management." This comes from Tim again. "A number of researchers have referred to bureaucratic management as a factor in corporate decline. Bureaucracy, however, is a complicated issue. Some researchers came out in strong support of the hierarchy, the strongest and most prevalent artifact of bureaucracy. The overwhelming view of most influential writers, though, is that bureaucracy has had its useful life and needs to be retired. A number of researchers referred to narrowness of vision in the management team as a co-producing factor in decline.

"And what about narrow vision?" Tim asks rhetorically. "Narrow vision refers to the habit of many organizations when promoting people to the next level of management because of their successful performance in a narrow vision functional area. Most senior staff and managers are very narrow in their focus. They're credible only in their own functional departments. These managers are better at operations management and tactical decision-making than at strategic and general management. Management teams of declining organizations are thus unable to keep pace with changes in the market place. Although accelerated change does not threaten a well-run company, failure to keep pace with change accounted for 25 percent of internal co-producer effect in decline."

"I have another one," says John, "Changes in market demand."

Everyone is really on a roll here. I feel good for the enthusiasm my team brings to the table towards our mission. John promptly identifies two types of decline market demands – secular decline and cyclical decline. "Secular decline," he explains, "refers to decline in the need for certain industries or product classes within industries, whereas cyclical decline refers to a decline linked to a declining business cycle. Secular decline takes place when fundamental shifts in economic patterns, social and cultural norms and political situations occur.

He continues. "The external producers of a financial crisis within a business are often the result of an overall decline in the industry in which the business is active. Economic slow-down, increasing competition, social change, and technological change are all possible external co-producers of decline."

"Wait a minute," says Carin. "Because I am the woman on the team, that doesn't mean I have less to say."

"To the contrary," Scott replies, a smile on his face.

Carin gives him one of her glares as she continues. "Another co-producer is the lack of marketing efforts. Without a marketing effort, the business will gradually become unknown and its products and services will not remain the first choice of the consumer. The vast majority of businesses in decline are characterized by an all-round complacency, not only among management, but also among employees at all levels, and particularly those involved in the marketing effort.

"The underlying problem in the lack of marketing drive is usually management. This state of affairs is characterized by...and, Scott, will you please list them for me?"

Scott picks up the marker and walks to the large paper pad.

1. A poorly motivated sales force
2. Non-aggressive management
3. Wasted advertising
4. Lack of targeted key customers
5. Lack of targeted key products
6. Poor after-sales service
7. Poor or total lack of marketing research
8. Outdated promotional material
9. Weak or non-existent new product development.

Carin pauses for a moment. We notice Scott does not write the notes as competently as Carin, but they will do.

She continues. "Financial gearing, cost of debt, and financial policy are all issues to be associated with corporate decline." Here she turns to Scott again. Would you please take these down?" As he nods, she continues, "There are at least three types of financial policies that can cause failure."

1. A high debt/equity ratio (high gearing)
2. A conservative financial policy
3. The use of inappropriate financial sources.

"As far as conservative financial policy is concerned, the lack of reinvestment in plant and equipment, a high dividend payout, and high liquidity and low gearing can also lead to decline," she concludes.

I stand up and look at all the lists posted around the room.

"This was a good day" I say. "You've done some excellent research. Let's get together tomorrow morning at 10 o'clock. That will give us time to see how our departments are doing before we continue here."

chapter 5

ON WEDNESDAY MORNING I start the day by saying, "I have found that not many researchers have defined the stages of decline. But there are seven stages of corporate crisis." I refer to the notes that I have already written and placed on the tripod.

Stage 1. The firm is in a strong position with little competition. It develops systems, management practices, and a culture that depend on a few capable leaders. The management style is a combination of autocratic, directive, and paternalistic.

Stage 2. The firm grows and becomes more complex. Competition increases and new technology emerges. The firm now needs strong and capable leadership. It does not, however, have enough people with these skills because many people with good leadership potential left because of the frustrations created in Stage 1. However, the firm's performance does not deteriorate dramatically. It remains well placed in its established markets. It lives off its reputation.

Stage 3. Declining performance leads to a focus on short-term results. Internal tensions lead to conflict, which cannot be handled constructively. Senior managers seem incapable of facing these tensions, and so functional policies, rather than corporate policies, prevail. The firm lacks a coordinated strategy. This undermines efforts to improve the quality of management.

Stage 4. The firm's management reaches crisis denial. At the initial stages of crisis development, the management team was not even aware of the impending crisis, often due to lack of adequate control systems and poor management information. Now when the crisis is upon them, they deny it because they overlooked earlier signals.

Stage 5. The signs of the crisis have now become visible, but the management team rationalizes the symptoms and finds some lesser justification for them. This means they assume that there is no need for action and that they can continue along familiar paths. They're trying to keep the crisis hidden or buried.

Stage 6. Disintegration of the organization begins. As the crisis deepens, structures and processes start to disintegrate. Management at last realizes that a crisis exists. Managers take some action, but, given the requirements, not enough. Inflexibility is rampant, decision-making groups shrink, autocracy increases, secrecy grows. There is greater reliance on fewer people who support the prevailing wisdom. Opposing thinkers are ostracized.

Stage 7. Despite the management team's sending out messages about how "everything is under control," the organization eventually collapses. It becomes evident to all stakeholders that management is *not* in control. The process of disintegration involves a decrease in the number of decisions being made, a decline in commitment to organizational goals, and managers becoming more self-reliant. If recovery is to be achieved, dramatic action is now needed."

I look up from my notes. "The first three phases describe the phases of organizational development," I say by way of clarification. "According to this definition, crisis seems to be entirely embedded in leadership by only a few capable persons and a general lack of management skills during growth and expansion. The other four items in the list are a more realistic description of crisis, irrespective of the co-producers of the crisis. This list is therefore more applicable to all forms of organizational crisis." I look at the list again. "It is interesting to note how behavioral in nature both descriptions are," I conclude.

Now Tim speaks up. His binder is much thicker than it was just a few days ago. "I did a lot of research in the field of recovery interventions," he says, "and I want to share my findings with you. The fourteen major studies on corporate recovery (see #1 in the appendix) that I reviewed have followed a similar research methodology in that they studied primary information, some directly and others indirectly, and their findings are therefore comparable. All fourteen found specific intervention strategies or management actions that can be implemented to recover an organization in crisis.

"Three key turnaround elements, according to which

recovery actions can be classified, that I found are the following." He pauses, and then asks Carin if she can takes notes again. She agrees to do so.

1. Improving management processes. It follows that if management is the major co-producer of decline in 70 percent of cases, then improved management and management processes should be the fundamental recovery strategy.
2. A viable core business. Next to management and management process, the competitive aspects of the business are the most important determining factor in recovery.
3. Financial resource issues. Adequate bridging finance has to be secured. This means the company has to have sound relationships with bankers and parent companies. It also means the role of creditors in assisting in recovery must not be underestimated.

Carin is back at the large pad of paper on the tripod, trying to keep up.

Tim continues. "In one of the few truly international studies (see #2 in the appendix) sixty-five turnaround cases were examined. What made this study remarkable is the fact that in case studies conducted in the USA, Canada, Europe, Africa, India, and the Far East, the researchers found twenty-seven categories of management actions that were engaged in during the turnaround phase. A correlation coefficient of 0:44 between the rate of profit improvement and a company's total score on the twenty-seven actions was found. Therefore, the study indicated that the twenty-seven turnaround factors as a system were associated with improvement in profitability. The more of these factors used, the higher the rate of profit improvement."

At this moment, to Scott's delight, Linda walks into mission control. "Adam," she whispers, "sorry to disturb you, but Scott is needed in his department." I nod to Scott, who stands and follows her out the door.

"In a study (see #3 in the appendix) of the rejuvenation of mature businesses during the 1980's," I say, looking at my notes, "the first-stage renewal process pointed to the importance of a gradual progression of recovery activities until sustained profitability is achieved." I take out more of my notes and place them on the tripod "The four-stage rejuvenation process progresses as follows."

1. Galvanize. This involves creating a top team dedicated to renewal, an often-overlooked aspect of rejuvenation. Rejuvenation is not just fixing up a few problematic activities or functions, but changing every part of the organization and the way its various functions, territories, and groups interact. The CEO cannot achieve this task on his/her own. He or she needs to build a top team that can assist in all ways. However, creating this top team involves finding not only new members, but also galvanizing and synchronizing the team in terms of urgency, perception of the real problems, and understanding what future actions may be required.

2. Simplify. This means cutting out activities, removing outdated control systems, simplifying

the business, and concentrating scarce resources on a smaller agenda.

3. Build. This overlapping next stage implies building new advantages for later deployment. Starting with small experiments by individuals, those with positive results will grow to become corporate entrepreneurs with total functions and working across functions until they have transformed the business. This is also a phase of new learning.

4. Leverage: As the organization grows in competitive strength, it can now expand into new markets with new products and new parts of the value chain. Leveraging capabilities can be achieved through acquisition, alliances, or internal moves that can extend the company's newfound advantages to a much wider sphere of activities."

Walking back to my seat, I continue. "To rejuvenate itself, an organization has to move progressively through all four phases.

"Other studies used the method of indirect sourcing of secondary data, such as company financial and marketing information. Rather than studying the specific management actions taken to recover an organization, researchers were interested in the interactions of certain indices with each other and how these changed from before, during, and after the recovery. In a study of fifty-four U.S. businesses (see #4 in the appendix), areas looked at were:

- New products, marketing, price productivity, R&D
- Receivables, product quality, new plant and equipment

- Market share, direct costs, inventories, capacity utilization.

Three combinations of strategies were described in response to poor performance. Six of the companies studied followed a combination strategy of asset and cost surgery. Nineteen companies followed a selective product/market pruning strategy, while twenty-eight companies exhibited no clear combinations a state of affairs, which was described as 'piecemeal productivity,'" I conclude.

Now Tim speaks again. "The next stage was the generic intervention strategies, which included the convergence and divergence of research studies. A review of these studies indicates that turnaround management involves taking a set of specific actions or intervention strategies. Some of the actions identified (see #5 in the appendix) were confirmed through successive studies, and the regularity with which certain actions appeared increased the validity of these findings. A successful corporate recovery strategy consists of a number of generic turnaround actions and factors and the more of these are engaged in, the more successful the recovery would generally be. Here's a list of the generic intervention strategies identified by most influential researchers

1. Organizational design, development, and change. The conventional remedial action programs employed by most turnaround executives are not particularly successful because they reflect a very narrow base of personal experience. They do not sufficiently focus on organizational change, but include only reducing cost, increasing revenue, and refocusing product market.

Organizational change is not, however, merely an issue of changing the organizational structure. It involves the following ten tasks:

a. Creating a vision, establishing a set of values, making cultural changes
b. Creating relearning, incentives, motivation, training, meetings, committees
c. Making changes in organizational culture and schemes
d. Making changes in organizational design (decentralize, flatten the structure)
e. Making changes in decision-making processes
f. Making changes in communication structures
g. Making changes in budgeting and capital expenditure processes
h. Making changes in performance management
i. Making changes in financial control
j. Making changes in business processes and patterns of activity.

Carin's hand is flying across the pages as she writes. Tim lets her catch up and catch her breath, and then continues.

2. Reasons for organizational change. One of the reasons why organizational change and development are important aspects of a recovery strategy is that, as soon as the organization is too large for the new CEO's mindset, behavior, and values to impact all the members of the company, the turnaround process slows down. Development actions are then needed throughout

the organization to perpetuate this impact. Team building in particular becomes important.

Organizational change should not be contemplated as a short-term strategy except under special conditions. These special conditions would be in the case where change is required to facilitate divestiture or to gain management control, such as widening the span of control at the top end of the organization.

Real progress can only be achieved by making people perform differently inside the organization. Rejuvenation is generated from within.

3. Restructuring. In most of the cases the organizational structure almost always moved away from centralization to decentralization. In decentralization, problems of internal growth might result from a failure to graduate from a centralized functional structure to a decentralized product division structure.

In addition to decentralization and often to facilitate it, there is a tendency for recovering organizations to flatten their structures by eliminating layers of management. Most turnaround practitioners flatten their organization, removing as many as three to four layers of management. This is done, not only to reduce costs, but also (mostly) to create a more hands-on approach, streamline information flow and decision-making, and improve coordination and the mobility of resources.

Along with flattening the structure, most of the recovery companies that were reviewed (see #6 in the appendix), not only implemented wider spans of management, but also cut out or reduced unproductive head office staff functions. Head office specialists in staff functions, such as planning, human resources, training, marketing, and public relations, are seldom worth their cost and at best, only second-guess operational executives. They do not really add value.

4. Culture of empowerment and entrepreneurship. Once a company realizes that the human capital in the organization is its most valuable asset, systems and processes must be designed to maximize the productivity and value of these assets.

The most valuable asset of a successfully run company is the ability of its people at all levels to use their knowledge, creativity, and experience to generate ideas. For turnaround, a process or system should be created to maximize the generation of ideas. The process should be clearly understood by all employees and rewards should be attached to ideas accepted and/or implemented. In a study of rejuvenated organizations, in contrast to mature, stagnant organizations, certain attributes, or capabilities discernible in organizations that have achieved the status of what is termed "corporate entrepreneurship" were defined. The distinguishing features were teamwork in all parts of the organization, aspiration to achieve more than the immediate task, experiments to explore what is feasible, the building of capabilities to learn and adapt and, finally, recognizing and resolving dilemmas.

5. Change of management. There is wide agreement regarding change of management, in that ten of the fourteen studies found change to be necessary

to make a turnaround. These ten studies all argued that most firms in crisis also suffer from bad management, which further reinforces the need for a new top management team. Existing management is seldom capable of taking the drastic action that recovery requires. Because poor management is one of the most important co-producers of decline, new management seems to be the solution.

At this point, we all look up as Scott walks back in and takes a seat. "My apologies," he says.

Tim gives him a nod and continues. "When we look at the reason for change of management, we find that dramatic action is necessary to turn an organization from a loss situation to a sustainable recovered position where financial performance compares well with or exceeds that of its competitors in the same market.

"Ideally, a company should embark on a recovery program *before a crisis develops*, or at least before it becomes too severe. But a crisis is often necessary to create conditions for unlearning and initiating change. Corporate collapse during a crisis is often a necessary catalyst for changing our paradigm. The general belief once was that when organizations chose strategies not in line with their industry "recipe," then they might fail. Organizations have often rejuvenated themselves by creating new organizational contexts different from their competitors' recipes when operating within a given industry. The creation of new context is associated with sustained rejuvenation.

"The purpose or importance of the organizational context

or schema is that it helps management to make sense of events and actions, guides comprehension, and enables them to map the experiences of the organizational world. By accepting institutionalized schemas, an organization member acquires trustworthy formulas to use to obtain desirable consequences when handling situations and solving problems."

Just as we are digesting this important information, Linda walks in again. "Adam," she whispers, "you are needed in reception."

I don't want to leave, but I must. "Please continue," I say as I head out the door of mission control.

Tim resumes. "The problem with incumbent management is that they often do not see the problem! A key question to ask in turnaround research, then, is who actually triggered the turnaround stage. This lack of recognition of the problem was associated only with *failed* attempts at recovery.

He smiles and looks at his notes again. "In only five of twenty-two cases studied (see #7 in the appendix) the board of directors of the parent company was among the first to recognise the failure and institute action. In one case, the external auditors alerted the shareholders to the impending crisis. In five other cases, banks and creditors triggered the turnaround phase. In three cases, the stockholders triggered it. And in the remaining cases, recovery was initiated by other sources, such as trade unions and the press.

"No clear trend emerged as to who would be most likely to realize that the organization is in trouble and initiate the turnaround. What is clear, however, is that it is hardly ever the incumbent management." At this everyone nods and smiles. We're seeing a significant trend here.

"The incumbent management of a declining organization

is frequently the last to admit that there is a crisis," Tim continues. "The longer the incumbent management takes to admit the severity of the problem and initiate action, the greater the likelihood of the turnaround strategy slipping into the control of external agents. This is not the only reason why a change of management is required. Managers who are more accustomed to 'normal' business conditions usually lack an adequate understanding of the special techniques and competencies required to accomplish a turnaround. As a consequence, many such efforts fail. Where the existing management attempted to recover the company, they used too few intervention strategies, and those they did try were not adequately implemented.

"When looking at the new chief executive officer," Tim continues, "we find that inadequate management, particularly at the CEO level, along with poor financial control, may be the two most important causes of decline, especially in the manufacturing industry. In a case study of twenty-two recoveries (see #8 in the appendix), it was found that in all, except two, a new CEO was appointed. In seven of these cases, the new CEO was an insider; in twenty others, outsiders were appointed. Among the twenty-two companies, there were twenty-seven changes in management – some of these because there was more than one change in the CEO position.

"The appointment of a new CEO is also a symbolic act. It's a new beginning. The new recipe brought in by a new CEO with a proven track record is always the safest because at this point there is not much time available for relearning. This new person with a proven track record is also in a better position to motivate a demoralized workforce."

At this point, having put out a small fire (so to speak) in

the lobby, I return and find that Tim still has his captive audience.

He gives me a small wave and continues, "When it comes to the question of whether the new CEO needs industry experience related to the business in crisis, we have found that many of these generic recovery strategies do not require an in-depth knowledge of the specific industry. A general, in-depth knowledge and understanding of management is probably more valuable."

He returns to his long list of items.

6. Business redefinition: Nine of the fourteen studies reported this as one of the intervention strategies a redefinition and change in the nature of the business, such as establishing a viable core business, diversifying, rationalizing the product line rationalisation, or refocusing on the product market.

Redefining a business is, however, a radical and complex attack on deep-seated profit problems. The strengths that are essential to the survival and success of a business often become blunted and cease to contain any critical quality. The following twelve actions have been mentioned as part of a process used to redefine a business."

Tim turns to Carin. "Can you make notes here?" he asks her. With a sigh, she returns to the tripod.

a. Addition or deletion of products
b. Addition or deletion of customers
c. Changes in sales mix by focusing on specific markets and customers

d. Complete withdrawal from a market segment
e. Entry into a new market segment
f. Reduction in the breadth and the variety of models in the production line
g. Improvement in design discipline
h. Refocusing advanced engineering products
i. Consolidation of production in one plant
j. Pruning educational or technical services that are not valued by key customers
k. Choice of scale of operation
l. Choice of channels of distribution.

We all wait as Carin finishes the list. I must remember to tell her that she is doing a stunning job. Not one that, I am sure, she relishes.

Tim continues. "Business redefinition often involves a return to basics, a return to the core business and developing competitive strategies to differentiate the business from its competitors. Successfully recovered organizations stay close to their market niches during stabilization and use their marketing opportunistically.

"This is why strategies that solidify market niche positions are essential. It becomes necessary to define the boundaries of the currently served market and to consider the exclusion of customers that–" he ticks the list off on his fingers:

1. Are too costly to serve
2. Are located geographically too far from the business
3. Require an excessive amount of nurturing
4. Have quality standards that which cannot readily be met.

He turns to us and smiles. "Sales people can then identify and focus on profitable customers and profitable orders.

"After the business has been redefined," he continues, "and it has a new role within the chosen segment of the market, another dramatic change it must make lies in its functional policies and the behavioral patterns of its people. That is to say, the business now has to become aggressive in its niche. In turning a company around, it is not sufficient to develop a radical business strategy; it is also necessary to adopt radical functional programs and to challenge current policies and work practices. There is simply no time for half-hearted and incremental moves. Powerful efforts at organizational change should follow business redefinition."

He turns another page in his copious notes and returns once more to his long list.

7. Improved marketing/revenue increase. Companies that are characterized by poor management rarely have a well-developed marketing plan. Management of the sales force is often weak. Sales targets, call patterns, leadership, and control are virtually nonexistent.

"Where a firm is very close to the break-even point, simply cutting costs might remedy the problem. Those who operate well below their break-even point, however, must be ambitious and concentrate on income and revenue generation as a strategy. Where markets are declining, the task is then to identify new markets.

Following are the seven most common elements of improved and more aggressive marketing during turnaround:

a. Improved Selling
b. Increased advertising
c. Improved pricing
d. Lower prices
e. Product market refocusing
f. Product introduction and reintroduction
g. Product changes.

8. Cost reduction. Seven of the fourteen studies reported cost-reduction activities as part of a successful turnaround strategy. These activities might involve cutting operating budgets and reducing staff levels.

The aim of cost reduction as a strategy tool is to improve the organization's cost position relative to its competitors. It is also an operational tool used to improve productivity.

But when it involves massive retrenchments, we must be cautious about its harmful effects. The cost-cutting strategies of many so-called turnaround artists can best be described as *stripping measures* that often sacrifice the quality of the product or operation of the business. Although they may be required in specific cases, these strategies are often the result of over-zealous turnaround teams that are searching for a quick, simple fix to a very complex problem. The tendency of managers in troubled companies is to become reactive. Unable to see the real problem, they merely do more of the same. Adopting a short-term financial focus is another area to be careful of.

An interesting finding is that retrenchment, diversification and liquidation of fixed assets, and technological innovations can be decelerators that actually slow down the process of recovery.

9. Technological changes. Most of the studies see technological change as part of an overall recovery strategy. This includes innovation, new product development, new manufacturing methods, and increased efficiency.

10. Strategy development. Five of the fourteen studies mention some form of strategy development when reference is made to diagnosing, planning, problem-solving, and balancing the immediate future with the long-term future.

11. Financial control. It is interesting to note that although lack of financial discipline was cited earlier on as a major co-producer to corporate crisis, only five of the fourteen researchers saw it as part of an overall recovery strategy.

Nothing is more important to a successful turnaround than cash. Cash management, in the form of cash flow projections, control of capital and operating expenditure, and management of accounts receivable, inventory, and accounts payable, becomes critical.

12. Investment, Only four of the fourteen studies referred to investment in plant and equipment as an intervention strategy. This investment can include modernization of existing plant facilities and increases in efficiency.

13. Growth strategies. Only three of the fourteen studies referred to growth strategies or acquisition

with the aim of increasing revenue. It can therefore be assumed that in some cases, a growth strategy may be feasible, yet not generally critical. It is not prevalent in recovery situations.

Growth via acquisition is generally considered to be a surprising recovery strategy because over-acquisition is often one of the causes of decline. Acquisitions are most commonly used to turn around stagnant organizations and boost financial performance.

14. Debt restructuring. Of the fourteen studies, only three reported significant debt restructuring or the raising of additional finance as a strategy. Organizations in crisis are often overgeared and must reduce their debt/equity ratio. This can be achieved by restructuring debt, by signing new agreements between the business and its creditors, and by converting interest and debt into negotiable financial instruments."

Out of breath and at the end of his notes at last, Tim finally sits down. I can see that he is pleased with his report.

"Good work, Tim," I say, and the others applaud. "Let's end the day on that note. Get a good night's sleep, everyone, because tomorrow we will start off by hearing from Scott regarding the types and phases of turnaround."

chapter 6

IT IS NOW THURSDAY morning, and as we gather in mission control, it looks as if John had a long night. Did he have any sleep at all? We wonder, but commence with our literature research in our mission to find out what the competencies and strategies of turnaround or recovery executives are.

Scott is first to take the floor. "Various researchers have identified a number of different types of turnaround," he begins, then he turns to Carin and asks, "Can you please pin these sheets with the classification, indicating convergence and divergence of the different views to the walls?" He turns to us and says with a smile, "I prepared these last night so Carin can relax a bit." Carin beams as she pins the first list to the wall.

"In our discussion of these different types of recovery

approaches," Scott says, gesturing at the lists, "we should note that none of them are pure in the sense that they cover different intervention strategies to the exclusion of others. Among the wide range of strategies used in recovery approaches, some elements of the overall recovery strategy need far more attention than others."

Now he looks at the lists of types of turnaround and reads them off.

1. Management process turnaround:
    - non-surgical transformational
    - strategic turnaround
    - management process turnaround.

2. Surgical reconstruction turnaround:
    - Surgical/reconstruction turnaround
    - Surgical/productivity and innovation turnaround
    - Asset/cost surgery turnaround
    - Piecemeal productivity turnaround
    - Operating turnaround
    - Operational turnaround.

3. Marketing innovation turnaround:
    - Non-surgical innovation oriented turnaround
    - Product/market pruning turnaround
    - Marketing turnaround
    - Product breakthrough turnaround.

4. External agent turnaround:
    - Economic/business cycle turnaround
    - Competitor environment turnaround
    - Government-related turnaround.

5. Unclassified – financial turnaround.

Scott gives us a minute to digest these lists, and then continues.

"Another turnaround is the management process turnaround. This primarily involves issues such as changes in strategy and changes of direction that lead to restructuring of management processes and the culture of the organization. It also involves organizational redesign, changes in top management, motivation of staff, and enhanced management control. It can, however, also include diversification, marketing related actions, and increased efficiency and productivity.

He nods at the next list. "The surgical reconstruction turnaround focuses primarily on asset and cost surgery. Also important are significant retrenchments and divestiture, improvements in production capacity, increases in productivity/efficiencies, and increases in revenue. Other aspects are diversification, changes in top management, restructuring, incentives and motivation, and innovation and product development.

"The marketing innovation turnaround," he continues, "focuses on aspects such as product markets refocusing the reassessment of existing products along with the total image of the company. Other concerns are leveraging assets to create growth, innovation, and other marketing related actions and new product development and breakthrough. Diversification and changes in top management also belong to this approach.

He turns to the next list. "The external agent turnaround includes all turnaround situations where the recovery results more from favorable changes in the external environment than from internal changes in the company. The economic/business cycle turnaround involves improvements in economic conditions. The competitive environment turnaround, which includes competitive price increases, and government-related turnarounds, which involve changes in government procurement policies, are caused by major shifts in regulations or direct government assistance."

He turns to the next list. "The financial turnaround primarily involves debt restructuring, financing, and (to a lesser extent) cost control and other such measures. No support for this unclassified approach could be found and so it will be left as unclassified."

He takes a sip of water and turns to Carin and asks her to list the items he reads next. She nods and he continues.

Researchers found four types of recovery situations falling into two classes, as follows:

1. Non-recoverable turnarounds:
   - No-hopers. Despite attempts at recovery, they fail. These businesses are characterized by decline in their core business, indivisible assets (such as one plant), high fixed costs, and a fast decline in demand.
   - Short term survivors. Recovery returns them to profitability, but they eventually go insolvent again due to an inability to develop a sustainable competitive advantage.

2. Recoverable turnarounds:
   - Mere survival. Recovery attempts are partially successful, but due to industry characteristics and limited resources, the company remains at

low levels of returns.

- Sustainable recovery. This means successful implementation of recovery strategies enabling the organization to achieve above average financial performance in the long term. This type of recovery is difficult to achieve, particularly where the business has a weak product-market position in its core business.

Suddenly the tripod where Carin is writing collapses with a thud. Scott stops abruptly.

"Well," she says, exasperation clear in her voice, "I *am* doing the best I can."

Scott rushes over and returns the tripod to its original position. As he hands her the marker, he clears his throat. "OK," he said with a weak smile, "let's continue." With another sigh, Carin says she's ready.

"When looking at the various approaches," he says, "we might ask ourselves which recovery approaches are the most successful. The review of the literature indicates the various approaches that may be followed in the recovery of a business organization. The logical next question, therefore, is which approach is *preferable*?"

He pauses to make sure we are all following him. "A contingency view suggests that the most preferable approach is probably the one that is most in line with the nature of the particular crisis. Indeed, there cannot be one mode of turnaround for all kinds of corporate sicknesses. Which co-producer triggers which category of turnaround management? Twenty causes, or co-producers, were correlated with the twenty-seven turnaround elements in forty-two cases of complete recovery. Only one co-producer was related to a number of turnaround elements or activities. With the exception of adverse market conditions, the rest of the eighteen co-producers of decline did not correlate significantly with the twenty-seven turnaround elements, which suggests that the design of a turnaround strategy is not influenced by the nature of the co-producers of decline.

"Sixty-five cases were further classified into four categories (see #9 in the appendix). The rate of profit improvement for turnaround types was studied as regards non-surgical transformational, non-surgical innovative, surgical reconstruction and surgical productivity, and innovation, as shown in the first list I presented this morning. The effect of each of the turnaround approaches was determined by measuring the profit growth (return on sales from year to year) from the moment the new CEO took over and the beginning of recovery actions until the business reached a break-even point. The time it took to recover ranged from less than one year to four years for both types of non-surgical turnarounds and from less than one year to eight years for surgical turnarounds. The average number of years it took was just over one year for non-surgical turnarounds and just under two years for surgical turnarounds.

"For complete recovery, that is, at least four percent profit on sales, which often takes longer than just break-even, the average of the surgical turnarounds was four years. For the non-surgical turnarounds, the average was two years. The management process turnaround seems to be the most successful. The best results are obtained by non-surgical turnarounds, with significant participation of internal and external stakeholders. This involves strengthening the organization through management processes and systems and corporate integration. This is, however, in addition to the core turnaround activities, such as change of management, changes in product portfolio, aggressive marketing, and restructuring for greater accountability. The most successful recoveries resorted to significant organizational change in terms of structure and processes. Failed recoveries made little or no attempt at organizational change. Further support for this conclusion states that in a survey of eighty-one turnaround executives, the management process turnaround was cited as the most prevalent and most successful. It was, in fact, considered to be the only 'real' turnaround.

"As far as the universal applicability of turnaround approaches is concerned," he pauses to consult another page of his copious notes, "different views exist, on the one hand concluding that the recovery strategies used in the UK did not differ significantly from those used in the other countries, especially the USA, and on the other hand, maintaining that there can be no universal turnaround format because various types of turnarounds exist, each with its own formula. Concerning the type of recovery approach to follow for a particular company or for companies in a particular country or economic system, the research suggests sufficient universality of successful intervention strategies across all these variables."

We have a lot to digest here. Fortunately, Linda arrives with a tray of sandwiches, so our stomachs will be as busy as our brains for the next hour or so. "Thank you," everyone tells her, and we all help ourselves to sandwiches, chips, and hot coffee. Now the only sound in the room is chewing. The team is obviously pondering Scott's solid research and its ramifications in the real world. I suspect that we will also be talking in the halls and around the water coolers and via e-mail. Eventually, Scott signals to us that he is ready to resume.

"When we look at the stages of turnaround," he says, following Linda with his eyes as she goes out the door with the empty tray and food containers, "some of the studies that I reviewed proposed certain stages of corporate recovery. If we integrate these various views, we are led to the formulation of five stages of recovery. We must remember, of course, that forcing the myriad of actions it takes to recover a business into five stages is to deny the complexity of the issue. Not all the stages of the various researchers correspond exactly, nor do the stages have distinct beginnings and ends. There is a large degree of overlap, and some stages can at times run concurrently.

"A case for a 'critical stage' (see #10 in the appendix) was made as a distinct stage in the recovery process. This critical stage falls between the decline and the beginning of the recovery. During this stage, certain initial actions are often taken that may be contrary to the longer-term strategy of the company but necessary for its survival. The objective here is not yet turnaround. The critical stage is thus neither short-term nor long-term, but rather immediate-term. In the immediate term, the focus is not on revival, but on halting the failure.

"Then we find an evaluation stage that has been identified by a number of researchers (see #11 in the appendix). The evaluation stage involves creating a top team dedicated to transformation. It formulates solutions and action plans and communicates these strategies. This initial stage comprises a mixture of assessment and action. Analysing company problems is the key element and immediate survival the objective. As more literature is reviewed, it becomes evident that the establishment of a new executive team straddles a number of these stages.

"Another stage I found discussed in the literature is the emergency stage. This is when executives do what is necessary to survive and gain control. The aim in the emergency stage is to stop the outflow of cash in the form of purchases, accounts payable, appointments of staff, salary increases and interest payments.

"Some researchers advocate reducing the complexity of the business in terms of the number of products/services it offers, the number of markets it serves, and the number of operations it undertakes. Simplification also includes cutting out internal complexity, such as elaborate control systems, too many layers of hierarchy, and tortuous procedures. In the initial stages, most rejuvenators focus on only three dimensions: the product-market-scope, the information control system, and prioritizing tasks for key managers. The researchers also mention the formulation of a vision at this stage.

"Another stage is the strategic change stage. The researchers assert that, having eliminated the obvious losses and expenses, the next step is to achieve acceptable returns on sales, assets, and funds invested. The emphasis here is no longer on survival but on performance in the longer term. Four issues now become important: (1) profitability, (2) operating efficiencies, (3) creating a platform for future growth, and (4) development activities, such as building a new executive team, organization development, institutionalization of the new culture, and the motivation and upgrading of staff.

"Finally, we come to the growth stage. Once profitability

has been restored, financial control has been gained, and a healthy operation has been established, the organization can begin to look at leveraging its capabilities, long-term expansion, and growth through new product development and market development, as well as expansion and acquisitions. As the organization grows in competitive strength, it can again expand into new markets, new services, and new aspects of the value chain."

At this point, Scott very kindly pauses again to give us a few minutes to reflect on what we've just heard. Then he finishes his report.

"Very often," he says, "a company going through a crisis responds well to the initial stage of recovery and returns to profitability. But it does not reassess its business, and so it fails to implement strategies to prevent a future crisis. In the next downturn of the economic cycle, this company faces another crisis, and now it has fewer reserves than it had the first time around." He smiles as we all recognize this situation and nod our heads. "Securing effective change is laborious, and I've been reading about organizations that tried to short-cut the process. Most of them failed because they didn't alter their belief systems or failed to give people the skills and tools they needed to do the task better. In a few of the cases studied, which achieved industry leadership through their rejuvenation process, the turnaround took as long as a decade. There were no quick fixes." Scott finally stops.

It is now just after three o'clock. The sandwiches are long gone, we all have much to consider, and so we decide to break for the day.

"Tomorrow," I say, "John will report back on his research on the competencies of the corporate recovery executive."

"And, please," Carin says, "I implore you to seek another means of note-taking!" And with that, she slams the marker she's been writing with on the table and waltzes out the door as we men stare open-mouthed after her.

chapter 7

WHEN WE WALK INTO mission control on Friday morning, we find John already set up with an impressive looking PowerPoint presentation, which must have taken him hours to prepare. One thing I always enjoy is the competitiveness between my team members.

John's excitement about reporting on the managerial competencies required for effective organizational change, transition, and turnaround is evident. He begins almost before we've all taken our places around the table.

"In crisis situations," he says, "the ability to make decisions and implement new strategies becomes more critical than under normal business-as-usual conditions. The reason for this is the compressed time span within which fundamental, strategic decisions – which could lead to the total extinction of the organization – have to be made and implemented. This is further compounded by the fact that, unlike under healthy conditions, the recovery executive has to start at a low point in terms of the public image of the business, customer satisfaction, staff morale, negative culture, managerial competence, and limited and stretched financial resources.

"For a manager, the threat of a corporate crisis leads to stress, which in turn impairs his span of attention, time perspective, and flexibility. As a result, managers selectively filter information, rely too heavily on past experiences, lose their tolerance for ambiguity, start to stereotype, and focus only on short-term values. This process results in inadequate fact-finding and analysis and an inability to evaluate alternatives and their consequences or decide on a final choice of strategy. Where poor management is a co-producer of decline, the capacity of managers to cope with the growing crisis is severely impaired.

"Organizational change therefore needs a special kind of leadership. Current processes, policies, and procedures are disrupted and found to be inadequate. New systems have to be developed to cope with the changing demands of the environment.

The PowerPoint slide changes and John looks around at us as we regard the new information. "Leadership is a key factor," he continues, "in that organizational recovery has to take into consideration the complex issues of business redefinition and changes in organizational process and culture. Also needed are new organizational policies regarding assisting people in the organization to cope with the change and accompanying pressures and anxieties. The managerial competencies, personality, managerial style, and management practices of the individuals on the management team determine their response to the crisis. All these factors can co-produce either corporate recovery or further decline.

"Of particular importance," he says, "are the competencies and characteristics of the corporate recovery executive who is driving the turnaround from the position of CEO. The CEO influences the criteria according to which all new managers are hired and incumbent managers dismissed. He or she also influences the value system and culture to be established. These are all influenced by the reference point of their own competencies, personality characteristics, and personal values.

"When I looked at the concepts of managerial personality and competence, I found that a clear model, or framework, of managerial competence and its assessment was needed. This need stems from the very complex nature of managerial work and its interrelationship with the personality characteristics of the manager and his or her managerial effectiveness." Here John points to the bullet points on the slide. "The assessment of managerial personality, behavior, and skills is complicated by the vast differences in task and roles at various organizational levels, the differences in competencies required at these various organizational levels, and the complex nature of managerial skill or competencies.

"Much of what we know today is based on the thinking established in the early 1950s that behavior is a function of personality, primarily in terms of motivation or needs, as well as the situation or environment within which the person is acting."

The slide changes to a graphic of many colors. "The environment is represented as a field of forces that affect the person. Thus a person's behavior at any given time can be predicted if the person's needs are known and if the intensity and valence of the forces impinging on the person from the environment can be determined. An important implication for management and organizational changes is that if one attempts to change the behavior or attitude of an individual without attempting to change the same attitude or behavior in the group to which that person belongs, then the individual will become a deviant and come under pressure to get back into the line or be rejected. The major leverage point for change, therefore, is at the group level. It is necessary to either modify group norms and standards or bring in from the outside sufficient numbers of new executives with similar norms and values to create a critical mass to effect cultural change."

The slide changes again. "Researchers (see # 1 in the appendix) viewed job competency as an underlying characteristic of a person. It may be a motive, trait, or skill, an element of self-image or social role, or a body of knowledge that the person uses. Job competencies are underlying characteristics and, as such, can be viewed as generic. This means that the competencies may express themselves in many forms of behavior and across a wide variety of situations. Competencies reflect a person's abilities and lead to effective behavior. They determine what a person *can* do and not what the person *will* do.

The slide changes again and we see illustrations made with clip art. "Some researchers referred to type and level of competence. *Type* refers to behavior, such as initiative, analysis, etc. The types of behavior can exist at one of three psychological levels: (a) unconscious (i.e., motives), (b) conscious (i.e., self-image), and (c) social role level or behavioral (i.e., skill). A competency is more than just a skill or knowledge; it is a cause of effective performance.

"A *motive* can be defined as a recurring concern for a goal or condition that drives or selects behavior of an individual. An example of a motive would be the need for power. A *trait* is defined as a characteristic way of responding to a set of stimuli, for instance, initiative. *Self-image* is defined as a person's perception of himself or herself, whereas social roles refer to a person's perception of acceptable social norms. *Skill* is defined as the ability to demonstrate a system and sequence of behavior that is functionally related to attaining a performance goal.

"Behavior is, then, a response to a stimulus. In organizational terms, it's a response to a specific business or work situation or problem. Managers are constantly faced with situations and problems to which an appropriate response is required. This response can be categorized as managerial behavior, in that the stimulus elicits a specific group of responses, all focused on achieving a business result."

John stops as Linda appears in the doorway bringing in a cart laden with good things to eat and drink.

"Thank you, Linda," I say. "Team, let us take a moment to select a delicious morsel from this feast Linda has so efficiently put together."

Scott is first on his feet and in a flash is beside Linda, smiling and gazing at her adoringly. We all gather round the cart and make our choices, then move back to our seats. Linda exits the room. As we are finishing our lunch, John gives me a questioning look. I nod, and he stands up and switches his PowerPoint presentation back on. A new slide comes up.

"In terms of the environmental field forces," he says, "or

in a variety of situations, it becomes clear that the task of the CEO of an organization – and particularly a recovery CEO – induces unique environmental forces and variety of situations. In this regard, leadership is particular to a required role and circumstance." A new slide appears and John reads it to us.

"Cognitive complexity is central to, and is defined as, a function of the number of variables operating in a situation, the ambiguity of these variables, the rate at which they change, and the extent to which they are interwoven so as to necessitate their unravelling in order to see them. Executives therefore need to exhibit the cognitive capacity to deal with the requisite complexity of the system they have to manage."

As the next slide comes up, he glances at his notes. "The level of work an executive has to deal with can be measured in terms of the time span of discretion. The longer the time span of a role, that is, the maximum amount of time available to complete a task is, the greater its felt level, scope, responsibility and complexity are. Seven time spans were defined by some researchers (see # 1 in the appendix): three months, one year, 2 years, 5 years, 10 years, 20 years, and 50 years. These time spans correspond to the seven layers of management a large organization should have. For each upward shift in the stratum of task complexity, an upward shift in cognitive complexity is required of the requisite manager or leader. With the maturation of his or her cognitive capacity, the executive can grow to deal with increasing levels of complexity with a longer time span of discretion. It is the potential of the executive reflected in his or her cognitive complexity that determines managerial capability at any given time in a given role, and this capability can increase as the executive progresses from youth to adulthood, mid-life, and maturity. In order to understand the competencies, characteristics, and values of the recovery executive, let us first review the requirements of such a position."

The slide changes again. "Turnaround leadership involves the integration of the diverse and sometimes conflicting ideas of individuals with the internal and external requirements of the organization and its resources into a strategic business plan for the future. Managing change effectively requires the competency to create a new synthesis of people, resources, ideas, opportunities, and demands. Vision is essential, creativity is paramount, and systematic plans to provide for the logistics of resources are also crucial.

"One of the first, and probably the most important, requirements is for the CEO to create a vision of the new nature and direction of the business. Considering that business redefinition was identified as one of the intervention strategies needed to recover a business, then it follows that some visionary statement must be made by the CEO regarding the new nature and direction of the organization. It then follows that the CEO mandated to turn a business around must clearly demonstrate competence in creating such a vision.

"Given that organizational change was viewed by most commentators in this field as probably the most important intervention strategy in recovering a business, it is not surprising that many researchers supported the notion of having to create a new culture. It is required of the CEO to create an entrepreneurial culture that encourages its members to explore new ways of doing things, experiment with new ideas, and find new solutions to the current problems. This is a culture of innovative professionalism. An enabling empowered culture that has an open attitude to change needs to be established. In order to achieve this change, leaders need to continuously work with the values and the philosophy of the organization.

"Corporate recovery further has an organizational design requirement in that the CEO has to structure people within project teams and task groups in order to pursue the new initiatives of the organization and to show the team a clear and convincing route to the company's objectives.

"A further requirement mentioned is the ability to promote technological change and harness new technology for new product development and improved productivity."

Here John notices that our eyes are glazing over. "I only have eight more slides," he says. "Just stay with me, please."

As we all blink our weary eyes, shift in our seats, and bring our attention back to the slides, John continues. "The turnaround manager needs characteristics that are different from those required to run a healthy company. The particular personalities, behaviors, and values of the turnaround executive are crucial if we are to reverse the fortunes of a business.

"The required personal characteristics of the successful corporate recovery executive are listed on the following slides." And the next slide appears.

1. Competencies. Having defined the requirement for successful corporate recovery, the question is now what competencies the CEO should have to handle these situations effectively. A checklist of competencies could include:

a. The ability for visionary leadership
b. Convincing negotiation and communication skills
c. Entrepreneurial skills
d. Analytical and decision-making skills
e. Ability to prioritize
f. Ability to anticipate environmental changes
g. Ability to achieve results through others
h. Counselling and mentoring skills.

In reviewing the requirements for recovery, as discussed earlier, it becomes apparent that in addition to this list of competencies, the following competencies must also be requirements, and the slide changes again:

a. Strategic planning competencies
b. Organizational change competencies
c. Organizational competencies
d. Competencies in understanding and utilizing new technologies.

2. Personality characteristics. Although it is difficult to divorce personality traits from competencies because a personality trait is a co-producer of a competency, such an attempt would lead to a listing of the following traits that a recovery CEO needs to possess (next slide):

a. Initiative and enthusiasm
b. Determination and decisiveness
c. Creativity
d. Self-awareness
e. Objective orientation

---

    f. Impatience to get things done
    g. Flexibility.

In terms of social roles and self-image, the recovery CEO must furthermore be a:

    a. Completer
    b. Delegator
    c. Initiator
    d. Mentor and counselor.

3. Values and beliefs. In addition to specific competencies and traits, the turnaround CEO further needs to possess certain values, particularly:

    a. Social responsibility
    b. A boundaryless attitude toward every constituency – race, gender, workers, management, etc.
    c. A belief that people are the key to everything
    d. An external focus
    e. A relish for the customer.

4. Experience. Very little has been said about the experience of the recovery executive, other than his or her need to have a broad business experience and track record of having managed change."

Having finished the last slide, John finally comes up for air. He clicks off the PowerPoint screen.

Everyone in mission control, including me, is grateful that he has finished his presentation. "I am grateful," I tell him, "for the information we now have regarding the managerial

---

competencies required for effective organizational change, transition, and turnaround." It's time to change the subject, to get the team out of turnaround mode for a little while. "So what are you all up to this weekend?" I ask expectantly.

"Well," says Tim, "John and I are taking our kids camping."

"Adam," said Carin, "don't forget when you come on Saturday to have Helen bring that delicious salad that we all enjoy so much. And have the children bring their swimsuits. It looks like it's going to be a scorcher."

Carin and I were in school together and our families have been friends for many years. This will be one of those Saturdays when our families regularly get together.

"And so, Scott," I cautiously venture a wry smile, "any plans with Linda?" Scott returns a blank stare amid the others' chuckles.

"Well," I say, "that's it, then. Let's break until Monday. We'll start looking into the research methodology of our mission."

We all file out of mission control, leaving John behind to pack up his laptop.

chapter 8

IT IS MONDAY MORNING, and there is excitement in mission control. It is evident that all of us had a great weekend.

"Today," I begin, "we start a new chapter in our mission, defining the research methodology that we, as a team, are going to follow. Thereafter we will be going out and implementing this methodology ourselves in our different industries in practical ways.

"Before we set out, however, we will need to research and establish the methodology we will use during this mission. Before we can do this, we will need to do our due diligence on research problems studied in the social and business sciences. We will also need to examine the most prevalent research methodologies followed in the studies of corporate recovery and turnaround."

Seeing agreement on the faces of my team, I continue. "Starting today, we will discuss the literature and learn that the task of the social researcher is to express social phenomena as precisely as possible, considering their range and generality and the local and historical contingencies under which they occur. Social phenomena, like natural phenomena, appear or occur with regularity and stand in relation to each other."

Tim raises a hand. "In the world of social scientific research," he says, taking up the topic, "research design is more of a problem than in the world of natural sciences. In experimental research as it's usually done in the physical sciences, the researcher has control over the administration of independent variables and can see the competent effect on the dependent variables. In the social environment where social and economic phenomena operate, on the other hand, the researcher does not have the same control over conditions and variables. He has to observe these phenomena as they occur in their natural environment.

"Most social scientific research," he continues, "is based on non-experimental research, which is defined as a systematic, empirical inquiry in which the scientist does not have direct control of independent variables because their manifestations have already occurred, or because they are inherently not manipulable. Inferences about relations among variables are made without direct intervention from concomitant variation of independent and dependent variables.

"Since direct control is not possible, the researcher can use neither experimental manipulation nor random assignment of cases. Although it is possible to draw samples at random in non-experimental research, it is impossible to assign subjects to groups at random or to assign treatments to groups as in experimental research. Despite the weaknesses of the inability to manipulate independent variables, the lack of power to randomize, and the risk of improper interpretation of cause and effect, non-experimental research has to be used in the fields of psychology, sociology, education, and business because their research problems don't lend themselves to experimental research."

Tim pauses, turns on his laptop, and opens a PowerPoint presentation. "However, he says, "This was not seen as a weakness when viewed from a quantitative paradigm." Looking at the screen, we see the first slide, which reads, "Non-experimental social scientific research is divided into four categories." Tim clicks on "slideshow" and we follow along.

First, in the *laboratory experiment* that is a research study, the variances of all or nearly all of the possible influential independent variables not pertinent to the immediate problem of the investigation are kept at a minimum. This is done by isolating the research in a physical situation apart from the routine of ordinary living and by manipulating one or more independent variables under vigorously specified, operationalized, and controlled conditions. However, very few psychological or social phenomena, and hardly any economical phenomena, can be studied in this way.

Second, the *field experiment research study* is done in a realistic situation in which one or more independent variables are manipulated by the experimenter under conditions controlled as carefully as the situation will permit.

Third, the *non-experimental field study* is a scientific inquiry aimed at discovering the relations and interactions among sociological, psychological, and educational variables in real social structures. Scientific field studies systematically pursue relations, test hypotheses, are non-experimental, and are done in real-life environments like communities, schools, factories, organizations, and institutions.

Fourth, *survey research* studies small and large populations or universes by selecting and studying samples chosen from these populations. The aim of survey research is to discover the relative incidence, distribution, and interrelationships of psychological and/or sociological variables.

Tim switches off the PowerPoint, silently reads a page of his notes to get his ideas firmly in mind, then continues.

"For many years, scientific progress has been made in the social sciences through the application of a quantitative research methodology that has obvious advantages of verification and statistical manipulation of the data. As a result, acceptable conventions have been developed to aid the researcher. However, more and more researchers have shifted to a more *qualitative paradigm* because certain phenomena cannot be studied in any other way than with qualitative methods. Qualitative methods have thus emerged only recently as an array of alternatives to the mainstream quantitative methods. The expansion of qualitative investigation has been significantly advanced by the reformulation of their methodologies by 'hard-nosed' quantitative researchers who have now shifted substantially toward context-embedded qualitative inquiry.

"Organizational dynamics, one of many social phenomena, involves the study of how organizations change over time, how events across these time spans are linked, and what the processes and phases are by which organizations move from one state to another. These phenomena are often difficult to quantify. Quantitative methods have resulted in the study of only those phenomena that can be readily quantified, while other phenomena where only a qualitative approach will work are neglected. Qualitative research recognizes a complex and dynamic world in which the researcher's active involvement with the participants and multiple realities exist.

"There exist as a subset of organization dynamics the phenomena of corporate recovery and turnaround. This field of research concerns itself with the actions that co-produce corporate decline and the strategies that prove to be successful in recovering them.

"Studies that have attempted to identify management actions leading to turnaround have been confronted by two limitations. First, their qualitative nature has been criticized because these studies omitted any form of statistical evaluation and testing for significance of differences. Second, because researchers studied only publicly available information, it is difficult to infer what actions were actually taken by management to restore profitability."

As we all nod our understanding, Tim pauses to take a breath and a sip of water, then continues. "Studies of corporate turnaround have also been criticized for relying mostly on anecdotal and case data (see #12 in the appendix). More recent work in this field has compared successful and unsuccessful turnaround cases. These studies attempted to isolate the factors that co-produce corporate decline and recovery. The research (see #13 in the appendix) on corporate recovery and turnaround was criticized on the grounds that few researchers have examined the appropriateness of the performance measures they used to define decline and turnaround, which resulted in overlapping research populations and inconclusive results.

"The main problem in identifying the determinants of organization performance," Tim continues, "is one of antecedence. When a company performs well and possesses a unique feature, we cannot assume that this feature necessarily caused good performance. The reverse may well have been the case, in that it may be good performance that led to the presence of the feature, or that good performance created the conditions under which this feature could successfully exist.

"Unfortunately, due to the difficulty of tracking corporate events over a period of time, much organizational research has been cross-sectional or synchronic (at the same time) rather than longitudinal (long time) and diachronic (over time). More longitudinal and diachronic studies are needed so that we can better understand the patterns of cause and effect and the stimulus-response relationships in organizations. What appear to have been longitudinal studies were not necessarily longitudinal. In a study (see #14 in the appendix) of forty companies that had consistently performed well over a twenty-year period, evidence was never provided of any mentioned factor that was indeed present during only one of the twenty years.

"Attempts at longitudinal studies have been made. In an attempt to sequence events over time, studies (see #15 in the appendix) of past records of organizations were made using minutes of meetings, annual reports, and correspondence. Cases of decision-making in organizations were made to try to sequence events. From these studies, models emerged showing how organizational structures change over time, how transitions are handled, how culture changes over the organizational life cycle, how strategies are developed, and how organizations grow over time.

"The turnaround situation offers an opportunity to study social phenomena without many of the research limitations. Within the compressed time span of a turnaround, cause-effect relationships – or rather producer-product relationships – are easier to observe. Vigorous action usually precedes improvement in performance. In a turnaround situation, improvements in results are usually very noticeable. Random factors can therefore be ruled out, and it is easier in the study of turnaround to isolate the co-producers of organizational success.

"In order to improve on the research design on corporate recovery to date, the following six requirements need to be met." Here Tim turns his PowerPoint presentation back on and we follow the slides again.

1. Experimental and control groups should be used to prove clearly that actions taken and conditions created in recovered situations were different from non-recovered situations. This excludes random factors that may have been assumed to be associated with recovery success, but that may also be present in the non-recovery, or decline, cases.

2. Producer-product relationships should be established through the use of longitudinal rather than cross-sectional studies.

3. The data on observed events, processes, actions and strategies should, as far as possible, be reduced to a quantifiable form. This will allow for the testing of the significance of differences.

4. Rather than studying only publicly available information or impersonal secondary data

(statistics on research expenditure, advertising expenditure, assets in relation to turnover, and so forth), the actual management actions taken to recover the organization should be studied and examined on a first-hand, personal basis.

5. The companies selected to form part of the study sample should be selected on the basis of the same criteria, e.g., lack of profitability, return on assets, or any other criteria, and should be included on the basis of their similar natures and the severity of the problem.

6. Observations should be associated with a criterion of organizational or business success.

"All of these limitations," Tim concludes, "seem to summarize the state of scientific design of research studies we have reviewed for our research methods." He exhales deeply and takes a long drink of water.

"Good job, Tim," I say, then I look around the table to see if anyone has a question. When no one raises a hand, I begin with a few of my own. "What about the questions to be addressed?" I ask. "What about the method with which the companies in need to turnaround will be researched? How will an attempt be made to circumvent the above mentioned limitations?"

Carin waves a hand and opens her laptop. "I suggest the following research questions," she says. She turns on her own PowerPoint presentation.

1. What are the personality constructs, preferred managerial style, and values of the successful turnaround manager?

2. What are the behavioral competencies and cognitive capacity of the successful turnaround manager?

3. How does the successful turnaround manager structure management and organizational processes to co-produce the turnaround?

4. What major initiatives are taken and what intervention strategies are chosen to recover the business organization?

5. What is the effect of the personality, style, values, and behavior of the successful turnaround manager on the way in which he/she structures, first, the management and organization processes and, second, the actual recovery success?

Scott has suggestions, too. "For the sake of clarity," he says, "let us define the terms that will recur in our report on our research." With a wry smile, he starts up his own PowerPoint presentation and draws our attention to the following slides.

1. Chief Executive Officer (CEO). The executive chairman, deputy chairman, managing director, executive director, or general manager who assumes chief executive responsibility for the business organization and its performance.

2. Top executive team. Those executives who report directly to the CEO. Generally, these are positions such as financial director, marketing director, operations director, manufacturing director, and so forth.

3. Financial/economic performance. The extent of

revenue growth, profit, profit growth, return on sales, and return on assets.

4. Inadequate financial/economic performance. The financial conclusion, based on the above-mentioned basket of indicators, that financial/economic performance is progressively decreasing from a low base in comparison to previous performance, inflation, industry indicators and other organizations.

5. Corporate recovery. A condition in which the business has been successfully restored to adequate financial performance after an experience of inadequate financial performance. This improved economic performance needs to have been progressive and sustained for at least two to three consecutive years.

6. Failure to recover. A condition in which the business is experiencing inadequate financial/economic performance over a number of years, again based on the basket of indicators, and the executive team has been unsuccessful in recovering the business. This inadequate performance needs to have existed for two or three years. One unacceptable financial year does not justify the classification of being in decline, unless this single year represents a major loss situation.

We all write down these definitions in our own notes, and then I get the team's attention again. "Now for the fun part," I say. "We need to decide on our research design.

"Research design has two basic purposes: (a) to provide

answers to research questions and (b) to control variance. The method of research must therefore be chosen, given the circumstances, to eliminate as much variance as possible and to observe as purely, and as much as possible without contamination, the variables under review. The mission we have and the universe within which they occur influence the choice of methodology.

"Our mission can be classified as a non-experimental study in which we will use a qualitative case method to investigate two groups of business organizations, namely, an investigation group and a control group. The investigation group will consist of companies that were successfully recovered, while the control group will consist of companies in decline or with stagnant, inadequate levels of financial performance. The dependent variables will be profit growth, turnover growth, return on sales, and return on assets. The independent variables will be the behavioral competencies, cognitive capacity, and personality of the CEO, the choice of intervention strategies, and the manifestation of organizational processes.

"Due to the nature of our mission and the limitations of our sample size, the best research methodology for our mission seems to be a qualitative research design. In our mission, we will use some of our previous customers as well as some new companies with whom we have good relationships. There is not a sufficient number of successful corporate turnaround executives in our customer or contact base to use as examples to ensure the validity of quantitative statistical methods."

I start my PowerPoint presentation here. "The reasons for classifying our mission as non-experimental field studies are as follows," and I click on the slideshow.

1. It will be non-experimental in that both independent and dependent variables will already have taken effect and executed their producer-product relationships.
2. It will be aimed at discovering the relationships between the economic performance of a company (independent variables) and social and psychological phenomena such as behavior, competence, personality, and choice of actions and processes governing behavior (dependent variables) of the executives within the company.
3. It will take place in the real social structures of a community. That is, we will study the *real business world*.
4. No independent variables will be manipulated. They already exist and we will simply record and note them *ex post facto*.

I close my laptop and continue. "The strengths of the field study are its realism, its significance, and its relevance to the problems of human existence and quality.

"The variables in a field study are larger and richer than in laboratory experiments, and the quality lies in the richness of potential for discovery. In advocating the qualitative research approaches which, of necessity, tend to be used during a field study, it is inductive (generalising) of the nature and theory generating and quality of people's experiences. The developing theory is primarily grounded in personal experience, and so the theory emerges rather than being simply a reflection of the researchers' *a priori* framework. As qualitative researchers, therefore, we will focus on the context and integrity of the material and we may use quantitative data, but we will not build the account entirely from this. We can't work from only quantitative data because people's experiences and the observations of the researchers mediate the object of study.

"The most serious weakness of the field study," I continue, "is its non-experimental nature, which weakens statements of relations. The fact that two variables are observed as having existed or taken place at the same time, or the one shortly after the other, says nothing about their product-producer relationship. This is the obvious strength of laboratory experiments. It's an issue of the validity of the qualitative, case study approach: How do we know that the turnaround actions that will be taken will indeed make the turnaround happen?"

I reply to my own rhetorical question. "When we compare the actions of successful recovery situations with the actions of declining companies, we can assess the contributions of various management actions to the turnaround. Where certain actions or initiatives of successful recoveries significantly exceed those of the control group, we see that such turnaround actions contribute to, or co-produce, the recovery."

The team members are nodding in agreement as I continue. "According to researchers, a second way to address the validity issue is to relate certain actions of recovered and declining companies to a criterion of performance such as profitability. A strong relationship between the criterion and the particular category of management actions tends to indicate that this particular aspect is associated with financial success."

I turn the page in my notes. Now I come to the practical planning of our task. "As far as cause-effect (producer-product) relationships are concerned, the compressed nature of the turnaround situation requires a longitudinal observation of four to six years to determine these relationships. We will handle this problem by using an investigation group and a control group. We will relate the observed variables to a criterion of financial and economic success.

"But this concern with validity holds only if viewed from a traditional quantitative stance. Ecological validity is achieved by making the research to fit the *real world*, which is necessary if the findings are to be extrapolated to a wider population than the sample and if the findings are to be generalized beyond the situation constructed by the researcher. To increase ecological validity, we must ensure that as many variables as are present in the real world are also present in the research setting.

"In our mission, then, the ecological validity will almost automatically exist in that the study of recovery of the selected business organizations will take place in their natural settings, where as many aspects of management recovery actions as can be recognised will be present. As qualitative researchers, we will overcome this limitation by describing and recording carefully meanings produced during the course of our research and how the research setting influenced meanings. Our concern, therefore, is more specificity than replicability. Ecological validity is sustained when the particular meanings of the research setting are explored.

"Another problem that might arise is the lack of precision in the measurement of variables due to the greater complexity of the real life situation. It is also difficult to eliminate sources of error and contamination that arise from variables not being studied. In this regard, we will develop a system according to which management actions and organizational processes will be classified and quantified. Furthermore, we will relate the observations of management actions and organizational process to a criterion of economic or financial performance.

"Now," I say, returning to my PowerPoint presentation, "the qualitative research design will have the following characteristics."

1. Data appear in words rather than numbers and are collected through observation, interviews, and extracts from documents or self-report questionnaires. Data are processed before they are used.

2. Analysis consists of three concurrent processes:
   a. Data reduction: selecting, focusing, simplifying, abstracting and transforming the raw data.
   b. Data display: organizing the information to permit drawing conclusions and taking action. Matrices, graphs, networks, and charts can be used to facilitate the display.
   c. Drawing of conclusions and verification: noting patterns, themes, and clusters.

3. Qualitative data analysis is an interactive process. Therefore, data reduction, data display, and the drawing of conclusions and verification take place at the same time and are continuously reinforced by each other.

Stopping to take a drink of water, I continue a moment later. "Qualitative research is part of a debate, not a fixed truth." Here I am gratified to see that the team is in agreement. "Normally, it is the representation of the meaning of a problem or issue. Research is an attempt to capture the sense of an issue, and researchers accept the fact that there will always be a gap between the things we want to understand and accounts of what they really are. Unlike in quantitative research, prediction and control are not relevant.

"Earlier on, we discussed six requirements that were needed to improve the research design of studies undertaken in the field of corporate recovery. Let us now consider the design of our own mission in relation to those six issues." Everyone around the table is taking notes now. These are serious researchers on my team. We will design our mission to meet the first requirement.

1. The first requirement was to use two groups in order to prove clearly those actions taken and conditions created in recovered situations which will be different from non-recovered situations.

2. The second requirement was that producer-product relationships should be established through the use of longitudinal, rather than cross-sectional, studies. In our mission, we will review the management actions taken to recover the organizations. We will monitor the organization over a period of three to five years.

3. The third requirement stated that the data on observed events, processes, actions and strategies should, as far as possible, be reduced to a quantifiable form, so as to allow for the testing of the significance of differences. In our mission, we will develop a system according to which management actions and organization processes

will be classified and quantified.

4. As far as the fourth requirement is concerned, instead of studying only publicly available information or impersonal secondary data, we will closely examine the actual management actions taken to recover the organization. In this regard, we will personally interview the CEOs of the organizations of both the investigation group and the comparison group. These interviews will yield first-hand accounts of management actions taken.

5. The fifth requirement was that the companies in the sample should be selected on the basis of the same criterion, e.g., lack of profitability, return on assets, etc. They should be included on the basis of the similar nature and severity of the problem. In our mission, due to the limited number of recovery and decline organizations that will be willing to participate, this requirement will be difficult to meet. Nevertheless, we will review all cases and compare companies according to the criteria of revenue growth, profit growth, return on sales, and return on assets.

6. The sixth requirement was that observations should be associated with a criterion of organizational or business success. We have already decided that this will be done. Our observations of management actions and organizational processes will be related to the criterion of economic or financial performance.

"In conclusion," I say, "although the field study is the closest of all types of studies to real life and therefore has no element of artificiality, it still has its own weaknesses. Nevertheless, discoveries by observation are as fundamental as those made by experiment, and both are important." I stop for a moment to stand up and stretch my legs. Following my lead, the others stand up, and two of them leave mission control for a minute or two.

When we're all settled again, I go on with my presentation. "We will also need to look at the criterion score. The researcher's most obvious concern is to maximize the experimental variance. The aim of our mission will therefore be to select business organizations for the investigation group that show dependent variables (e.g., financial performance) that will be considerably better than those of the declining or stagnant organizations in the comparison group. It is when we maximize the experimental variance that we can most easily observe differences, if any, in the independent variables – executive competencies, cognitive capacity, personality, intervention strategies and organizational processes.

"If differences in the independent variable are not significant and substantial, there is little chance of separating the effect of this variable from the total variance of the dependent variables, other than what is due to chance. The variance of a relationship must be given the chance to show itself separately from the total variance, which is a composite of variances arising from a number of other factors and chance. Unlike in most research studies, we will select the two groups of companies on the basis of the dependent variable of financial performance, rather than the independent variable of managerial competence and intervention strategies.

"Why? Because although financial results will be deemed to be dependent on managerial competence and choice of intervention strategies, it will be more feasible for us to select one group of high-performing companies to investigate and compare these companies with a group of low-performing companies. The dependent variable – financial performance – will be the criterion according to which we classify companies as successfully recovered (our investigation group) or declining (our control group).

I pause to search for and find another set of notes. I hold up a periodical. "In an illuminating article (see #16 in the appendix) on the performance measures of corporate decline and turnaround, sixteen turnaround companies were studied. Seven used some measure of profitability to define decline and recovery, three used return on investment, three used return on assets, one used market share, one used Altman's z-score, and one did not define a criterion measure.

"Fourteen of those studies used only one criterion, such as profitability. One used two criteria, such as profitability and return on investment, and one used more than two criteria, return on assets, return on equity, sales, and labor productivity. Because not all recovery cases are of the same severity and cannot be measured in the same way, we will be using the following typology for classification and measurement." I lay down the periodical and turn on my laptop again. The team follows my slides as I comment on them.

1. Imminent bankruptcy. This is a crisis turnaround situation in that the business is in danger of insolvency if immediate, radical action is not taken. The window of opportunity is only three months

to one year. An organization facing bankruptcy can show signs of recovery within two years. Typical measurement criteria include profitability.

2. Declining profitability. This is a cash-flow turnaround, where immediate action may be needed before long-term strategies are implemented. These organizations can show signs of recovery in about four years, from start to peak. Typical measurement criteria include profitability, but where profits are already positive, declining margins indicate the crisis.

3. Substandard performance. This constitutes a turnaround from mediocrity. The business has marginal performance problems. Inadequate performers need not have declined from previous profitability and are not classified as recoveries when there were marked improvements from previous performance. Typical measurement criteria include return on investment, return on assets, and profit returns in relation to industry.

4. Declining market share. The market share turnaround indicates a decline in market share, but does not necessarily go hand-in-hand with a lost situation. Turnarounds in market share are associated with a four-year period. Typical measurement criteria include declining sales/revenues in relation to the market.

5. Inadequate asset productivity. Asset productivity turnarounds are characterized by inefficient asset utilization, which can be recovered from a two to six year period. Typical measurement criteria

include return on investment and return on assets.

"In a study (see #17 in the appendix) of sixty-five recovery cases," I continue, ending the slideshow, "two criterion scores were used. The first was profitability, where a break-even position preceded by bad losses indicated a successful recovery. The second was rate of profit growth, calculated by taking the maximum loss as a percentage of sales and subtracting this from the profit as percentage of sales during the first year after break-even in which the business again made a profit.

"The reason that earnings on sales were used as a criterion is because these figures are readily available in most cases and are adequately reported. A criterion like earnings per share or return on equity, on the other hand, would be difficult to study, as this information is not always readily available, particularly for private companies or operating divisions of larger groups of companies.

"At the end of the day, then, the most basic and fundamental measure of the success of a business organization is whether its revenue exceeds its cost. Once this basic (and often crude) condition has been met, more sophisticated measures of economic success come into play."

I am just finishing when in walks Linda at noon with our lunch. Where did the morning go?

"Here," says Scott, jumping up and rushing over to Linda to take the tray from her, "let me help you with that."

Seeing grins around the table, I announce, "It's time to take a break and stretch our legs." Team members stand and gather around the lunch cart, chatting about this and that. We enjoy a hearty lunch, and then I reconvene the meeting.

"The best way for us as a team to complete our mission," I

tell them, "will be by using specific guidelines. Let us select four factors as the criteria according to which we classify the business organizations in our mission into investigation and comparison groups, or recovered companies versus declining companies." I write the following on the chalkboard:

1. Year-on-year revenue growth
2. Year-on-year profit growth
3. Return on sales: profit as percentage of turnover
4. Return on assets: profit as percentage of total assets

"When looking at sampling of companies," I continue, "researchers identified two basic types of sampling: probability and non-probability. In probability, or random, sampling, each individual has an equal chance of being included in the sample. In non-probability sampling, however, there is no way of eliminating the probability that an individual will be included in the sample. Non-probability sampling includes quota sampling, purposive sampling, and accidental sampling. As we know, much research uses non-probability sampling. People or events are often included in samples merely because they are conveniently there at the time of the research. Such samples are, however, biased and therefore have an impact on the statistical inference.

"In relation to our mission, the dependent variable— corporate recovery or decline in terms of historical financial performance—will not be manipulated. It will be *ex post facto,* that is, its history has already happened. Random allocation in the sample will thus be impossible.

"We will approach four companies that meet our criteria for corporate recovery and four companies that have failed in recovery. We must anticipate that since not all CEOs will find the time required by the investigation, not all companies we approach will agree to participate. This means we will study the first four turnaround companies that agree, along with the first four that have experienced inadequate economic/financial performance. Our selection of companies will thus be classified as a purposive sample. As far as access and availability allow, our companies will be matched according to economic sector. We will also strive to choose companies spread across various economic sectors or industries."

Noticing that John has something to say, I nod to him.

"As a team," John says, "let us decide to focus on the industries we're familiar with."

"Yes," I reply. "Good idea. We will make no attempt to match companies according to size, but rather to exclude companies with a turnover of less than $100 million per year and employing less than 500 people." Everyone around the table nods. They're already beginning to plan.

I continue. "We will study eight companies registered as public or private companies. They will be in the industry sectors of manufacture-chemical, manufacture-medical, retail-other, and services-freight. Four of these companies will be in recovery and four in decline, according to their industry/sector. The willingness of the CEO to participate and make approximately twelve hours of his or her time available will largely dictate our sample.

"Our investigation of each case will consist of three phases. Phase 1–assessment. Phase 2–survey of intervention strategies. Phase 3–survey of organizational processes.

"Phase 1, the assessment phase, will be an assessment of the CEO's behavioral competencies, cognitive capacity, and personality, preferred roles, and values. We will assess each of the eight CEOs individually during a four and a half hour managerial assessment procedure. This will be followed by a two-hour feedback session on the results, which will take place at a later date to allow time for interpretation. Confirmation as to face validity will be obtained by asking for each CEO's extent of agreement with the findings. Without exception, they need to agree as to the accuracy of the findings.

"Each CEO will be observed across a range of behavioral competencies, which will be recorded as they work their way through situations that I will describe below. We will interpret our observations according to generally accepted assessment practices and quantification according to a standard system.

"Next, we will translate observational information into raw scores. The raw scores for each behavioral competency and each trait will then be compared with a data bank of more than four thousand managers successfully employed across most industries and levels in business organizations. The data bank covers all levels of managers across all corporate functions across all industrial sectors except mining. The term "successfully employed" refers to the fact that each manager in the data bank will be, at the time of assessment, employed in a managerial position in a business organization.

"We can assume that these comparisons will result in profiles that give the percentile rank for each competency for each candidate. In this way, for each CEO, the degree of competence in dealing with each managerial situation will be expressed as a percentile rank, which indicates his or her relative competence compared to the managers in the data bank.

"During the managerial assessment procedure, each

participant will be subjected to assessment exercises that will serve as simulations of the executive role and task. The measure development competence will be in dealing with the following managerial situations:

- Problem analysis and decision-making
- General management
- Staff management.

"For each situation, we will look at case studies or managerial exercises that have been done before and/or evolved over a period of approximately fifteen years and have been administered to approximately four thousand managers at the time of our mission. From these, we will develop specific simulations.

"The first exercise, problem analysis and decision-making, requires (a) the ability to think conceptually about the problem, (b) the intellectual ability and creativity to formulate questions about the problem (analytical ability), (c) the ability to gather information and reason with the facts (reasoning power), and (d) the ability to come to a logical conclusion as to what action will solve the problem (anticipation).

"We might, for example, test a candidate on his or her decision regarding whether a hypothetical company needs to replace its production machinery. The manager will have limited time to prepare questions to be put to an independent resource person and a set time in which to ask the prepared questions or any other questions that come to mind. The manager will then be required to reduce the information to a conclusion and to make a recommendation.

The second managerial problem will be an in-basket exercise to assess his or her ability for general management:

the ability to initiate action (initiative), to understand the problem (managerial understanding), to make a judgment in terms of the consequences of the actions (consequences), to delegate (delegation), to give clear, decisive direction and leadership (decisiveness) to subordinates, and, last, to make sound arrangements. We will describe a hypothetical company and give the manager we're assessing fifteen issues that a general manager normally has to deal with on a day-to-day basis. These will include staff problems, customer complaints, cash flow problems, profitability issues, purchasing choices, operational concerns, and strategic choices, such as to import or to produce locally.

"The third management situation concerns staff management. We will assess each manager in terms of motivating subordinates (motivation), showing leadership in terms of setting objectives and giving guidelines and performance standards (direction), and being adaptable in incorporating a subordinate's ideas into joint problem-solving (flexibility). In this exercise, we will present a hypothetical situation where the manager will have to discuss with an employee unacceptable work habits, a customer complaint about bad service, and a feasibility study to be done. In a role-play situation, the manager we're studying will act as the manager and one of us act as the subordinate staff member.

"We have also learned that underlying the behavior observed in handling the simulated management situations is a thought process referred to as 'cognitive capacity.' The thought process underlying each behavioral manifestation can be classified according to which of seven strata it supports. This is similar to how the competencies are classified in terms of a raw score, and then translated to a percentile score.

"The following seven stratified systems of cognitive complexity in problem solving and decision-making that pertain to the business organization have been identified (see #18 in the appendix)." I turn everyone's attention to my PowerPoint presentation again.

1. Stratum one – the reasoning process of simple assertion within the cognitive world of symbols. Stratum-one workers do motor-visual work. They manipulate tools (motor) and co-ordinate this movement with visual capabilities (visual) to perform a task. An example is a hotel manager telling a waitress, "Jill, the guests on the patio would like some tea." There is no reasoning process and concepts involved, only the symbols of "tea" and "guests." Stratum-one people are concerned with doing a particular job.

2. Stratum two – the reasoning process of accumulation within the cognitive world of symbols. Stratum-two workers do elementary problem solving. They accumulate related facts, figures, or incidents to form an impression of a developing trend or problem. Based on this, they correct the actions of stratum-one workers and thus program and schedule stratum-one work. For example, a stratum-two person might say to Jill the waitress, "Before you serve tea, would you please ask Peter to fix the electrical supply? It tripped again." Stratum-two people are concerned with scheduling, programming, and problem solving.

3. Stratum three – the reasoning process of serial processing within the cognitive world of symbols. This is the first stratum of real operational management. Stratum-three workers go beyond just accumulating data to solving problems and predicting future events. They have to manage a series of sequential tasks over a longer period of time. For example, the manager of one hotel in a hotel chain has to manage the upgrading of that hotel because the stratum-one person cannot serve tea, and stratum-two worker cannot properly program repair activities until the stratum-three person manages the project of upgrading the hotel's facilities. Stratum-three managers are concerned with managing particular function within given parameters, such as policies, budgets, structures, and strategies.

4. Stratum four – the reasoning process of parallel processing within the cognitive world of symbols. Stratum-four contains elements of strategic thinking and managing a number of series of tasks in parallel. For example, the operations director of the hotel chain manages the serial upgrading of five hotels, plus a management development program and a pricing structure exercise. Stratum-four managers formulate the policy, strategy, and budgets within which stratum-three managers can manage the operation. They typically have to manage a number of projects at the same time and see the interrelationships among them.

5. Stratum five – the reasoning process of simple

assertion in the cognitive world of concepts. Unlike strata one to four workers, who deal with the clients, service, prices, lunchtime, food, drill, tea, etc., stratum-five managers start to deal with concepts like asset management, cash flow, market strategy, and decentralization. Stratum-five people are concerned with the survival of the total business organization as an economic and social entity and have to make quick responses, often intuitively, concerning pricing and strategy. Their role is to integrate the various functions into a whole or a business concept that can survive in the market place against competitors. The CEO of a chain of hotels is a stratum-five manager.

6. Stratum six – the reasoning process of accumulative processing in the cognitive world of concepts. Stratum-six managers accumulate information about their environment, for example, per-capita earnings, inflation, gross domestic product, empowerment, government policy, and fiscal and monetary policy. The accumulation of this information leads to defining emerging trends and problems, which in turn leads to actions to insulate their businesses from problems and create a synergistically integrated group of companies. An example of a stratum-six manager is the CEO of a group of companies or the chairman of several companies. She or he may, for example, decide to shift all future capital investments to stimulate growth and expansion in the group's agricultural businesses, sugar and citrus, due to greater export

possibilities and higher profit margins. Stratum-six managers create businesses, merge them, acquire them, and liquidate them.

7. Stratum seven – the reasoning process of serial processing in the cognitive realm of concepts. This is the highest stratum within the business world. A stratum-seven manager functions at a level higher than the chairmen of the boards of a group of companies. These are the industries at a very high conceptual level whose managers, through serial processing, plan and guide total industries and markets over decades. Examples include Anton Rupert, with his influence in the Tabasco industry world-wide; Harry Oppenheimer, with his influence on diamond manufacturing and marketing world-wide; or Bill Gates of Microsoft, who shapes the software industry.

I turn off my laptop again and pause to catch my thoughts. "On our mission we will use the Mann-Whitney U-Test to test for statistically significant differences between the groups in recovery and decline. It is important to mention that in all cases, we will use raw scores rather than percentile scores in statistical procedures.

"In Phase 2 of our mission, the survey of intervention strategies, we will conduct in-depth interviews with the CEOs. During these interviews with the recovery participants, we will ask them to describe in detail all the intervention strategies they have engaged in. These will be major initiatives that they and their top executive teams undertook during the recovery phase following their appointment to direct the company away from liquidation to survival and adequate financial performance. These initiatives will include key decisions taken, major strategies adopted and specific management actions taken to recover the business. In the case of declining companies, we will ask participants to describe in detail all major initiatives, key decisions, and management actions taken since the company started going into decline. This will cover a period of two to five years that the companies have been in decline. We will make careful notes during all of these interviews and on the initiatives, including how they were done, why, and what their effects were. These activities of the management staff of a company being studied will then be qualitatively clustered into categories of management actions.

"Next, we will attempt to make sense of the phenomena of the results of our research we have noted by grouping and then conceptualizing objects/actions/events that have similar patterns or characteristics. After we have defined the categories of management actions, we will analyze each case in terms of these categories. Specific actions per case will be allocated to these categories and the frequency of action per case per category will then be calculated.

"The companies that were successfully recovered will next be compared with those in decline in terms of their choices of intervention actions and initiatives put into operation as the proportion of management time spent or attention given to each intervention strategy. Where the scores of the successful recoveries significantly exceed those of the control group, we will interpret the scores to mean that those turnaround actions contributed to the recovery."

Here I pause again to catch my breath and make sure

everyone is keeping up. They all nod encouragingly, and so I continue with our third phase.

"In Phase 3, the survey of organizational processes, which will also be part of the in-depth interviews conducted during Phase 2, we will ask the participants specific questions about a range of critical organizational processes.

"This process will begin with the identification of variables that prior research suggests might be relevant to this mission and that the literature we studied indicates. This will include the eleven critical organizational processes that govern the behavior of the organization and its employees and determine its culture. For each process, we will determine specific criteria, as indicated by the literature, to be incorporated into a structured interview format. Then we will probe our participants as to the extent to which the processes in their organizations meet these criteria. Their answers will then be recorded and reflected in a three-point scale:

1. No manifestation of process. No evidence of the process or particular subset could be found. (1 point.)
2. Moderate manifestation. Some form of process exists, but in a relatively unsophisticated form and in line with the state of this process in most other cases. (2 points.)
3. Strong manifestation. Many actions, policies, and processes give a *gestalt* to the process. A high degree of sophistication exists in comparison with all the cases in both samples. (3 points.)

"After gathering the data from all eight organizations, we will assume that it will become clear to us that in some organizations there will be no trace, or manifestation, of certain issues. For example, some organizations will not bother to formulate a mission statement. This organizational behavior can be classified as *no manifestation*, and earn one point. In some cases the manifestation of a process, for example, 'scanning the external environment,' may be evident in terms of market research, but it might not be much different from what most of the other organizations in both samples do. Such a case will be rated as *moderate manifestation* and will be awarded two points. Where, however, the manifestation of a process exceeds what most of the cases in both samples will do, it will be classified as a *strong manifestation* and earn three points.

"It will be much easier," I conclude, "and probably more reliable, to use three categories. That's why the interview data we collect will also lend itself to a three-point scale."

At this point, Carin holds up one hand and points to her wrist watch. "Gentlemen," she says, "I am the mother of a four-year-old boy and one-year-old girl. I need to get home to my family! It's 6:50 p.m. I suggest we go home now."

I can't help but agree with her. It's been a long day. "Let us not spend any more of our time within the walls of mission control," I say. "Let's take the rest of the week to begin identifying the eight companies we'll be working with within our industries. We can meet again on Monday and report back." I close my laptop and stand up. "Thank you all for your hard work. Have a great weekend."

chapter 9

ON MONDAY MORNING, as I enter mission control I find Scott with his usual donut in hand and John looking, as always, as if he had no sleep. Today my team is ready to discuss the company to be studied, along with their key financial performance indicators. I let them finish their morning coffee before I call them to order.

"Each member of the team," I say, "will begin by identifying the recovery company and the declining company they will work with."

John stands up first and goes to the big whiteboard on the wall. He writes the names of his companies on the whiteboard.

1. Recovery company: Rubber, Inc.

Nature of business: Specialist manufacturer of rubber and PVC moulded and extruded products for the agriculture, building, footwear, mining and motor industries.

Status: Operating company listed on the stock exchange and part of a larger group of companies. Company is classified as a chemical firm.

General comments: Company was turning in losses. A new CEO was brought into the company to recover it. The new CEO took up this position in March, 2001, and is still the CEO.

Period of review: 2001–2007 (six years).

2. Declining company: Chem-Ag, Ltd.

Nature of business: Manufactures chemicals for use in the agricultural sector.

Status: Limited public company on the stock exchange in the economic sector of chemicals.

General comments: New CEO was appointed in January, 2002, through a restructuring exercise rather than a need for recovery or turnaround.

Period of review: 2002–2006 (four years).

Scott is second to list his companies on the whiteboard.

1. Recovery company: Freight, Inc

Nature of business: Freight management, including forwarding, clearing, shipping, agency, projects, and logistics covering operations in the U.S. and major European countries.

Status: Operating company, unlisted, part of one of the largest industrial groups in the U.S. The group is listed on the stock exchange. Company is classified under transport.

General comments: Company was experiencing losses, so the shareholders appointed a new CEO with the purpose of recovering the company.

Period of review: 2000–2005 (five years).

2. Declining Company: EXPAR, Ltd.

Nature of business: Express parcel delivery anywhere in the world. This company links up with other international express overnight delivery companies.

Status: Operating company, part of one of the largest industrial groups in the U.S. Listed on the stock exchange. For comparison purposes, categorized under the industrial sector of transport.

General comments: In this case, four directors of the company will be interviewed because the CEO was recently dismissed from his position due to losses in two consecutive financial years.

Period of review: 2001–2006 (five years). Note that 2001 will be chosen as a base year because this year was the beginning of the declining trend.

Third to list his companies on the whiteboard is Tim.

1. Recovery Company: WeSell, Ltd.

Nature of business: Retailing. Wide range of products. Clothing, food, liquor, household appliances, etc.

Status: One of the largest retail groups listed on the stock exchange. Company is classified under retail for industry comparisons.

General comments: As a result of lackluster performance, a new CEO was appointed to turn the group around. He took up his new position in July, 2001, and is still managing the group.

Period of review: 2000–2005 (five years)

2. Declining Company: Merch, Inc.

Nature of business: Mass merchandiser of a wide variety of consumer goods on a retail basis through a network of stores throughout the U.S.

Status: Operating company of a larger group of retail companies listed on the stock exchange. Company compared with retail sector.

General comments: The CEO who will be interviewed was promoted to this position in February, 2002, as a normal executive progression when the then-CEO resigned. He was previously the CEO of a smaller operating company within the same group.

Period of review: 2002–2006 (four years).

Finally, Carin lists her companies on the whiteboard.

1. Recovery Company: ChemCo.

Nature of business: Pharmaceutical company with direct sales force across U.S.

Status: Part of one of the largest pharmaceutical groups. Listed on the stock exchange.

General comments: After the company experienced losses, a new CEO was appointed in 2000 for the purpose of recovering the company and to restore it to profitability.

Period of review: 2001–2006 (five years).

2. Declining company: Pharma, Ltd.

Nature of business: Pharmaceutical company selling through a network of independent distributors throughout the U.S.

Status: Operating company. Member of a larger group of pharmaceutical companies listed on the stock exchange.

General comments: In this case, two directors of the company will be interviewed because the CEO was dismissed as a result of the loss situation of the business. He vacated this position in July, 2005.

Period of review: 2000–2005 (five years).

We all look at the whiteboard, where there are now eight

companies listed. Our sample groups are complete.

"We will," I tell the team as I stand up and walk around the table, "have to map out a plan regarding the gathering of the financial performance information for these eight companies so we can conclude which ones belong to the investigation group of successful recoveries and which must be classified as belonging to the control group of declining or stagnant companies. We will be researching the performance of all eight companies, plus industry information.

"We will also need inflation figures," I continue. "These transformations will be made to compare all revenue and profit figures across all eight cases to a level of 100 in year one. We will use the following scale to evaluate each case:

4 = exceptional progressive growth from year to year, outstripping inflation and other companies in the sample.

3 = positive growth above inflation and in comparison with other companies in the sample, but not as straight and progressive a line for score 4.

2 = no clear indication of a trend. Some years, low, others, a slight improvement.

1 = declining trend despite some good years.

0 = undisputed decline in curve or trend, ending in either a real loss in profit or a real negative growth in regard to turnover.

As the team members nod and make notes, I continue. "We will next determine the return on sales and return on assets. Return on sales (ROS) will be the actual operating profit for the year, divided by the actual turnover for the year, expressed as a percentage. Return on assets (ROA) will be the operating profit divided by actual total assets for the year, also expressed as a percentage. We will use the following scale evaluate ROS and ROA in each case:

4 = exceptional, straight-line growth in ROS or ROA from year to year to a level well above the industry norms.

3 = positive growth. Not as dramatic as for score 4, but still above industry norm or no significant growth. Returns are well above industry norms.

2 = no trend in terms of decline or growth and very much in line with the industry norms.

1 = returns show no clear trend but are below industry norms.

0 = declining or negative returns below industry norms.

"We now have a plan," I conclude as the morning ends for us. "Now that we already have permission and cooperation from the companies that each of you is reporting on, for the next eight months we will spend all of our time pursuing our mission. Our goal is to determine the strategies and competencies of successful corporate turnaround or recovery executives. Best of luck with your research," I conclude.

chapter 10

EIGHT MONTHS HAVE PASSED. We started in early spring and now it is winter. It is another Monday morning, and the team has come back together in mission control. As I walk through the door, I can already see the smiles on their faces.

"We did it!" Tim exclaims. "We have the information we were looking for to complete our mission. We're ready to report and discuss what we've been doing."

I am very pleased. "Your work will allow us to use our findings to help companies in declining situations. It will also help our company to add to our product line and services. Good work, all."

Our discussion takes up the whole morning. Our findings are given below.

Whereas in Phase 1 we did an assessment of the CEOs'

behavioral competencies, cognitive capacity, and personality, preferred roles, and values, during Phase 2 (the intervention strategies phase of the investigation) we interviewed the CEOs. During these interviews, we asked them to detail all the intervention strategies they used to recover their firms. These strategies comprised major initiatives, management activities, and/or strategies aimed at changing the order of things and giving new direction to recovering the company. In the declining companies, we asked the CEOs to describe in detail actions taken since they had become CEO or since the company started going into decline.

We asked each CEO to list or discuss all the intervention strategies or major initiatives that he (they were all male) and his team undertook within a given time frame. This process was somewhat projective, in that it probably reveals as much about the CEO's perceptions, mindsets, and views as it does about the actual activities he engaged in. Each CEO talked about the initiatives, activities, and tasks that he viewed as relevant and noteworthy. It is possible, of course, that there might well have been actions taken that the CEO failed to mention because according to his perception, these actions were neither major nor interesting.

In our presentation of the results of these interviews, the major initiatives taken in each case will be listed in order in which they were raised and communicated by the CEOs. The results of these interviews are given in Tables 1 and 2. The major initiatives taken in each case are listed in the order in which they were raised and communicated by the CEOs. Only actions that had a specific behavioral manifestation and were observable by others were considered. Furthermore, the only actions listed are those intended to recover the company or prevent further decline.

As the team spent eight months studying the management actions across all eight cases, clusters, or categories, of activities started to emerge. We found that eleven of these clusters emerged when activities were grouped according to the intention underlying the activity. We classified these eleven clusters as intervention strategies, each including a set of similar activities or initiatives. (The eleven strategies are listed following these explanatory paragraphs.)

Having established these eleven clusters of intervention strategies, we then analyzed each individual case. All management actions per case were allocated to the eleven strategies of recovery. Allocation of an action to a cluster of strategies was based on a qualitative evaluation of the action or its underlying intention in the context of the problems in the business.

Our next step in our analysis of the data was to attach a quantitative value to each action taken by a management team. In most cases, one action counted one point. Multiple occurrences of one activity, such as the appointment of four new managers, would add up to four points. In the cluster "Building the executive team," as seen in the eleven intervention strategies, for example, each project team or meeting also counted as one activity introduced.

As far as possible, one management action or initiative was allocated to just one cluster or strategy. Occasionally, however, an action could contribute to two clusters, particularly where the underlying intention was twofold. For example, when a manager was appointed to head up a newly created division of strategic importance, this action would count one point toward "Building the executive team" and one point toward

"Organizational design."

The eleven intervention strategies were used, by the team, in order of the frequency with which these activities manifested in the companies that were successfully recovered. The reason we use this sequence, rather than a sequence according to content, is that it reflects the real nature of this phenomenon as it occurs in its natural environment.

The eleven intervention strategies are listed and described as follows:

1. *Building an executive team.* This cluster includes activities aimed at putting together a management or executive team that can mange the company successfully. It also includes coaching and monitoring activities and management development program. Although this kind of activity typically gets referred to as "change of management," It includes far more than simply a change of management. It means building an executive and managerial team that, over and above the mere change of management, requires the strengthening of the team by appointment of new talent with new competencies from outside, promotions, reorganization, and team building.

2. *Integration.* This cluster includes any activity aimed at facilitating coordination and communication, breaking down hierarchical departmental barriers, and shifting communication from vertical to horizontal or from segmented to integrative. These activities involve the creation of network structures superimposed on the hierarchical structure through

the formulation of a range of interdisciplinary and interdepartmental task forces, committees, or meetings. This strategy emerged as a distinct cluster of activities that can be considered a subset of organizational development but is dealt with as a fully-fledged body of activities in its own right.

3. *Organizational design.* This cluster includes activities aimed at streamlining the organization, such as delayering and decentralization, reorganizing departments, strengthening and expanding, and adding or eliminating functions within the organization. It further includes redefining executive jobs, refocusing executives' time and attention, clarifying roles, and allocating decision-making powers. Elements of a recovery strategy can be defined as "organizational change" or as "restructuring."

4. *Performance management.* This cluster of intervention activities sets specific performance standards, either globally on a corporate basis or for individual executives or both. It includes formulating certain goals and instituting systems of measurement, a profit improvement program, job grading, performance measurement, and the development and implementation of reward systems and incentive schemes to reinforce successful behavior. It also includes performance appraisals.

5. *Philosophy, culture, values.* This cluster includes activities intended to establish a set of values and a culture governing the behavior of all members

of the organization. These activities include a strong element of education, attitude change, and setting behavioral standards, but can extend as far as exposing people to different ways of thinking and devising different scenarios for working and achieving goals.

6. *Financial discipline.* This cluster includes all activities aimed at restoring discipline in financial matters – improving systems of authorization and control; improving management of revenue, expenditure, and cash flow; and managing assets, maintaining margins, and gaining better control of credit.

7. *Cost reduction.* This cluster combines activities aimed at reducing the cost structure of the company, such as reduction in head count, sales of assets, reduction of interest rates, freeze on salaries, and so forth. In the cases reviewed for this study, retrenchment programs were embarked upon with the purpose to reduce costs, hence their being clustered with a seemingly unrelated issue like divestiture.

8. *Product-market focus.* This cluster includes actions aimed at repositioning the business in its market segment – conducting market research and portfolio analysis, changing product lines, refining or creating market image, opening new divisions to tap into allied markets, selling businesses that have no synergy with the core business, and buying into companies already operating in different markets.

9. *Increasing revenue.* This cluster includes all

activities aimed at getting more business and growing turnover figures. They are essentially of two classes: (a) expanding current activities by increasing production capacities, including issues such as exports and vertical integration, and (b) growing revenue through acquisitions and mergers and expanding into new business activities.

10. *Strategic development.* These activities focus on the implementation of strategic planning processes and the development of specific strategies to achieve specific aims. They differ, however, from the other clusters in that these are simply key decisions or processes, rather than specific activities. These activities include formulating a mission and vision and implementing strategic processes and specific strategies regarding revenues, cash flow, and cost reduction.

11. *Restructuring and rationalizing manufacturing or operational processes.* This cluster includes activities such as adopting systems of quality control and safety. It also includes eliminating products with short runs and high cost structures, installing better capacities, and redefining operational processes, productivity studies, and process re-engineering.

When we have finished discussing the eleven strategies, I say, "I have asked my assistant, Jenna, to help with posting the results of your work on the walls of mission control as you report back. What Jenna will post on the wall here will be two tables showing the quantitative results of this study, first for the recovered companies, then for the declining companies.

In these tables, the actual frequency of management actions taken or initiatives instituted are presented by case for each intervention strategy. For each intervention strategy, the proportion of management action, in respect of the total number of actions taken is also presented. This was calculated by taking the frequency of each intervention strategy, and dividing it by the total number of actions initiated.

"First, let's look at the frequencies and proportions of activities for the eleven clusters of actions across the recovery cases."

(see Table 1 at end of chapter)

"Let's take note," I say as they examine the table, "that the first figure denotes the proportion and the figure in brackets denotes the frequency of the action." The team continues to stand around the posted table and read and discuss it.

After a few more minutes, I ask Jenna to post the second table on the wall.

"This table," I say, "shows the frequencies and proportions of activities for the eleven clusters of actions across the declining cases."

(see Table 2 at end of chapter)

As the team stands before the second table, I say, "The frequency of intervention activities per case varied greatly," I continue, "and although this may in itself be important, the initial focus of analysis is the proportion of activities per intervention strategy to the total number of activities. The first figure in each cell indicates the proportion, and the second in brackets the raw score."

Finally, Jenna posts a third table, the frequencies and proportions for recovered companies and declining companies, next to the first two tables. "This table is also," I explain, "presented the rank-orders of the various strategies based on the proportion of occurrence.

(see Table 3 at end of chapter)

"The differences between these rank orders," I continue, "highlight the relative importance of the strategies as used in the two samples. The Spearman rank-order correlation of 0.20 between them was not significant, indicating the lack of similarity in approaches. However, the proportion of activities per cluster in itself is not necessarily an indication of its importance. As an example, product-market focus in the recovered companies accounted for a proportion of only 0.06 of all activities. Very little time and effort was therefore invested in this strategy, yet it could have been critical in terms of its co-producer effect. Furthermore, as indicated earlier, we should remember that these frequencies also reflect the CEO's view and mindset in terms of what he viewed as important in running the business.

"This also indicates that in terms of the intervention strategies with the highest rank orders, the two groups differed quite substantially. Apart from building an executive team and an organizational design, recovered companies spent much more time integrating, managing performance, and establishing a philosophy, culture, and set of values than declining companies, which, on the other hand, focused much less on these efforts. Most of their work went into increasing revenue, reducing cost, and restructuring operations.

"Recovered companies spent only 0.04 of their time on cost reduction, 0.01 on increasing revenue, and 0.02 on restructuring operations. This represents only 0.07 in total. Declining companies, by contrast, spent 0.42 of their time on these strategies. Recovered companies spent 0.34 of their time and effort on integration, performance management, philosophy, culture, and values, but declining companies spent only 0.08 of their time or effort on these issues. In order to test the significance of the differences between the means of the two samples in the frequencies and proportions of activities of actions across the recovery and declining cases, the Mann-Whitney U-test was applied. The calculations were carried out on the proportion and frequencies for each case. The statistical significance for sample size of cases is as follows:

TABLE 4. LEVEL OF Statistical Significance

LEVELS OF SIGNIFICANCE	U-SCORE
0.01	7
0.02	9
0.05	12
0.10	15

After the team has considered this information, I say to them, "Let us continue tomorrow at 8 a.m. with the U-values and their levels of significance for each of the eleven intervention strategies."

With that everyone stands up and leaves, leaving me to switch off the lights.

TABLE 1. QUANTITATIVE RESULTS, Recovered Companies

STRATEGY	JOHN'S COMPANY	SCOTT'S COMPANY	CARIN'S COMPANY	TIM'S COMPANY
BUILDING AN EXECUTIVE TEAM	.23 (8)	.29 (12)	.50 (19)	.19 (5)
INTEGRATION	.23 (8)	.21 (9)	.0 (0)	.04 (1)
ORGANIZATIONAL DESIGN	.09 (3)	.17 (7)	.18 (7)	.19 (5)
PERFORMANCE MANAGEMENT	.09 (3)	.0 (0)	.08 (3)	.27 (7)
PHILOSOPHY, CULTURE, VALUES	.03 (1)	.0 (0)	.16 (6)	.23 (6)
FINANCIAL DISCIPLINE	.12 (4)	.07 (3)	.03 (1)	.0 (0)
COST REDUCTION	.03 (1)	.05 (2)	.0 (0)	.08 (2)
PRODUCT-MARKET FOCUS	.03 (1)	.14 (6)	.05 (2)	.0 (0)
INCREASING REVENUE	.03 (1)	.02 (1)	.0 (0)	.0 (0)
STRATEGIC DEVELOPMENT	.06 (2)	.05 (2)	.0 (0)	.0 (0)
RESTRUCTURING AND RATIONALIZING MANUFACTURING OR OPERATIONAL PROCESSES	.06 (2)	.0 (0)	.0 (0)	.0 (0)
TOTAL	34	42	38	26

TABLE 2. QUANTITATIVE RESULTS, Declining Companies

STRATEGY	JOHN'S COMPANY	SCOTT'S COMPANY	CARIN'S COMPANY	TIM'S COMPANY
BUILDING AN EXECUTIVE TEAM	.00 (0)	.38 (11)	.29 (6)	.00 (0)
INTEGRATION	.00 (0)	.00 (0)	.00 (0)	.00 (0)
ORGANIZATIONAL DESIGN	.00 (0)	.21 (6)	.38 (8)	.07 (1)
PERFORMANCE MANAGEMENT	.06 (0)	.00 (0)	.10 (2)	.14 (2)
PHILOSOPHY, CULTURE, VALUES	.00 (0)	.00 (0)	.00 (0)	.00 (0)
FINANCIAL DISCIPLINE	.00 (0)	.00 (0)	.00 (0)	.14 (2)
COST REDUCTION	.07 (1)	.07 (2)	.09 (2)	.07 (1)
PRODUCT-MARKET FOCUS	.14 (2)	.03 (1)	.00 (0)	.14 (2)
INCREASING REVENUE	.71 (10)	.10 (3)	.14 (3)	.22 (3)
STRATEGIC DEVELOPMENT	.00 (0)	.03 (1)	.00 (0)	.14 (2)
RESTRUCTURING AND RATIONALIZING MANUFACTURING OR OPERATIONAL PROCESSES	.07 (1)	.17 (5)	.00 (0)	.07 (1)
TOTAL	14	29	21	14

TABLE 3. FREQUENCIES AND Proportions, Recovered Companies and Declining Companies

STRATEGY	REC	REC	REC	DEC	DEC	DEC
	FREQ	PROP	RANK	FREQ	PROP	RANK
BUILDING AN EXECUTIVE TEAM	44	0.30	11	17	0.17	9
INTEGRATION	18	0.12	9	0	0.00	1
ORGANIZATIONAL DESIGN	21	0.16	10	15	0.17	9
PERFORMANCE MANAGEMENT	20	0.11	7	4	0.08	7
PHILOSOPHY, CULTURE, VALUES	13	0.11	7	0	0.00	1
FINANCIAL DISCIPLINE	8	0.06	5	2	0.04	3
COST REDUCTION	5	0.04	4	6	0.05	5
PRODUCT-MARKET FOCUS	9	0.06	5	5	0.05	5
INCREASING REVENUE	2	0.01	1	19	0.29	11
STRATEGIC DEVELOPMENT	4	0.03	3	3	0.04	3
RESTRUCTURING AND RATIONALIZING MANUFACTURING or operational processes	2	0.02	2	7	0.08	7

chapter 11

IT IS A VERY COLD Tuesday morning. Nothing is stirring outside, and we're grateful for air conditioning in our building. Everyone is on time, including Jenna, who will help us again today.

I call the team to order. "First," I announce, "we will discuss the values of proportions. After that we will examine the raw scores.

"During the data reduction," I continue, opening my notes, "every management action or initiative was counted as one point and allocated or clustered in an appropriate intervention strategy. However, particularly in the case of declining companies, some of these initiatives actually had negative consequences or flew in the face of sound organizational or managerial principles derived from the actions of recovered companies we found in the literature.

"Raw scores were computed by taking the actual frequency per intervention strategy from the frequencies and proportions for both recovered companies and declining companies and dividing the frequency by the number of cases per group to give the average number of actions per case. zThis was the result of the Mann-Whitney U-values indicating levels of significance for differences in proportion for two groups across eleven major intervention strategies."

Here I ask Jenna to post today's first table on the wall.

(see Table 5 at end of chapter)

"This was the result of the Mann-Whitney U-values," I say, pointing to the table, "which indicate levels of significance for differences in raw scores for two groups across eleven major intervention strategies."

At my nod, Jenna posts the next table on the wall.

(see Table 6 at end of chapter)

The team gets up and studies these two tables, and then we sit down again and discuss the results shown on them. As far as proportions and raw score are concerned, the recovered companies differed significantly from the declining companies on three intervention strategies, "Integration," "Philosophy, culture, values," and "Increasing revenue." We also see, however, that when the data are adjusted for quality and actions with negative consequences are discounted, the proportions and raw scores change to the extent that "Organizational design" and "Restructuring and rationalizing manufacturing or operational processes" now also indicate significant differences. The two groups, therefore, differed in their use of five intervention strategies.

After our lunch break, we decide, we will discuss each of the intervention strategies. We will compare not only the results of the two groups of companies, but draw comparisons across all cases. I ask Jenna to post the list of strategies again, and then I read from my notes on the strategies and encourage discussion.

1. *Building an executive team.* The results indicate that according to the U-values, there were no significant differences between the two groups on raw score proportions.

"We can conclude," I say, "that building the executive team is not a differentiating strategy in terms of determining successful financial performance. It is the strategy recovered companies engage in because they have to solve a profit problem. Declining companies, however, also engage in these activities to virtually the same extent. A significant amount of management time and effort, probably the largest amount, goes into building the executive team. It could well be that in terms of quality, recovered companies made more right decisions than wrong ones, whereas declining companies made more wrong decisions than right ones. For instance, we might speculate that in replacing, for example, a sales manager, a recovered company filled the position with somebody significantly better. A declining company, by contrast, did not necessarily succeed in finding a better candidate but simply a replacement.

"It is further interesting to note that, although in terms of proportion of activities there is no significant difference, the recovered companies collectively had a raw score of 44 management actions for this strategy, which gives 11.0 managerial changes per case, whereas for the declining companies, a raw score of 17 gives 4.2 managerial changes per case. We can thus deduce that recovered companies were far more active in building their executive teams than declining companies were, and were more inclined to correct executive performance through replacements and dismissals than declining companies. However, the difference was not significant when the Mann-Whitney U-test is applied.

"Most of the studies we reviewed earlier indicated that changes in management are necessary," I add.

John speaks up. "Management starts receiving pressure when profitability plateaus or declines." Everyone nods in agreement.

"However," I continue, "when losses and huge write-offs are experienced, the pressure for new management mounts." Everyone agrees with this statement. "And where these losses or write-offs threaten the survival of the business, an inevitable change of management follows. New CEOs replaced virtually all the incumbent senior executives, but most of these new CEOs kept the existing management in the belief that they would perform better under new leadership. We have found that while a change of management seems to be a strategy in recovering a business organization, it does not preclude the possibility that many companies in decline may also show a high level of activity in this area."

We look at the next item on the list.

2. *Integration.* A significant difference was found between the recovered companies and in all measurements contained in the significance for differences in proportion and significance for differences in raw scores.

"Companies that had been successfully recovered," I say, "were found to have initiated more action in terms of integrating their organization than declining companies. The CEOs of recovered companies actively attempted to move away from a pure hierarchical structure. They breached inter-departmental and intra-company barriers by building networks of multi-disciplinary taskforces and committees and holding frequent meetings. They also initiated other actions aimed at improving communications and creating a sense of shared commitment to the company's survival.

"Creating an integrative structure can be seen as an initiative or strategy taken by the CEO of a recovered company to return the company to successful financial performance. Declining companies, however, are characterized by hardly any attempt to create integrative structures. This indicates a significant difference in what recovered companies focused on and how they emphasised a different way in which to run and manage their organizations.

3. *Organizational design.* Purely on a frequency basis, and not taking the good judgment or consequences of the activity into account, we found no significant difference between the recovered companies and the declining companies.

"However," I say, "when the quality of such actions was considered, differences did appear. Declining companies were characterized by changes in organization design that were not well thought through. CEOs later had to make further changes to the same departments or divisions to rectify the inadequacies of the first changes.

4. *Performance management.* With respect to the proportion of time and effort spent on managing performance, the Mann-Whitney U-test did not indicate a significant difference between the two groups.

I continue reading from my notes. "We found that the recovered group exhibited many more management actions regarding the management of performance and that declining companies, on the other hand, took fewer managerial actions focused on setting performance standards and rewarding staff in creative ways.

"Performance management as an autonomous and separate element of recovery strategy was not defined in most of the influential literature. Researchers who made some reference to performance management included it under the broader heading of organizational change. However, despite the lack of significant differences between the two groups, our investigation provides sufficient evidence of performance management as a distinct process managed by the executive team of a company in recovery.

5. *Philosophy, culture, values.* We also found a significant difference between the recovered and declining companies in proportions and raw scores for the U-values.

"The CEOs of recovered companies spent significantly more time establishing a culture than the CEOs of declining companies, who hardly did anything in this regard," I say. "Establishing a culture accounted for a proportion of 0.11 of their time and effort. Expressed in another way, in terms of time and effort invested, it was the fifth most important strategy of the eleven strategies. We can conclude, therefore, that although establishing a culture does not take up a major portion of the recovery team's time and effort, it is nonetheless critical, in that establishing a philosophy, culture, and value system proved to be one of the most significant differences between the two groups of companies.

6. *Financial discipline.* No significant differences existed between the two groups of companies in this regard. Although this is not a significant difference, it shows that recovered companies employed more intervention actions to restore financial discipline than declining companies did.

7. *Cost reduction.* No significant difference existed between the two groups in either proportions or raw scores in terms of the U-values for cost reduction strategies.

"It can be noted," I say, "that declining companies employed more cost reduction strategies in terms of the reduction of head count, sales of assets, and other cost saving measures than successfully recovered companies. Since these differences do not seem significant, however, cost reduction is not a determining strategy in turning a company around from lackluster financial performance. In fact," I say with a smile, "it was the declining companies that did more of it."

8. *Product-market focus.* There are no significant differences between the two groups in terms of product-market focus.

I look down at my notes again. "Contrary to other research findings indicating that product-market refocusing is a major intervention strategy in corporate recovery, we found no such evidence in this study. In one of the few studies where recovery elements were actually correlated with rate of profit growth, a negative correlation between profit growth and diversification and product rationalization, which forms part of this cluster of intervention strategies, was found (see #19 in the appendix) However, in term of their employment of this strategy, no difference between the recovered and declining groups of companies was found by our research.

9. *Increasing revenue.* A strongly significant difference between recovered and declining companies in terms of increasing revenue was found. The Mann-Whitney U-values for raw scores and proportions for quality indicate that declining companies initiate far more action in an attempt to increase revenue figures than successfully recovered organizations.

I turn to my notes again. "While we can speculate that recovered companies successfully generated revenues and could then relax in this regard, this is an unlikely deduction. Our examination of recovered companies started at the lowest ebb of their financial fortunes and included a period where lackluster performance and losses were experienced. Even at that stage, they did not initiate major actions to recover revenue levels.

"The findings of our study – that revenue-increasing activities were more prevalent among companies in financial crisis and were used to a lesser extent by those that recovered successfully – are unique. This could well indicate that a

CEO's preoccupation with revenue-increasing activities and neglect of organizational integration, design, and cultural issues can actually lead to future decline.

10. *Strategic development.* There is no significant difference between the two groups of companies in terms of strategy development. Successfully recovered organizations spent about the same amount of time on strategic development as declining organizations did.

11. *Restructuring and rationalizing manufacturing or operational processes.* The declining companies initiated much more action and spent more time in restructuring operational and production processes than the recovering companies. In terms of raw scores, declining companies initiated more actions to restructure processes than recovered companies.

I look up from my notes. "Let us summarize before we end the day. Managers have been defined as 'people who do things right' and leaders as 'people who do the right things.' But these simplistic definitions don't tell us what the right things *are*."

I look around at my team and ask three questions. "What are the right things to do when we are confronted with the task of turning a business organization around? What should the priorities of these recovery executives be? What should they spend their time on?"

I answer my rhetorical questions. "The results of our study indicate that individual executives of recovering companies do play a role in this critical phase of organizational life, and it's one that brings about a dramatic reversal in the fortunes of their organizations. The significance of these findings lies in the recovered companies' choices of intervention strategies, the activities they engage in, and the issues on which they choose, or choose *not*, to spend their time. There are also significant differences in perceptions and views as to what is important to do and what is unimportant enough to leave alone.

"The results suggest that the CEOs of successfully recovered companies tended to utilize the following intervention strategies to a larger extent than CEOs who managed declining or stagnant companies:

1. Integrative activities
2. Establishing a business philosophy, culture, and values
3. Organizational design.

"On the other hand, compared to CEOs of declining companies, successful CEOs tended to de-emphasise the following elements as parts of their recovery strategy:

1. Increasing revenue
2. Restructuring production and operational processes.

"Regarding the following intervention strategies, recovered companies did not differ significantly from the declining or stagnant companies:

1. Building the executive team
2. Performance management
3. Financial discipline
4. Cost reduction

5. Product-market focus
6. Strategic development.

"Of these six latter elements," I conclude, "it is important to note that although no statistically significant differences were found in terms of proportion of total activities, the successfully recovered companies did show more activity in the area of building an executive team, performance management, and financial discipline, and less activity in the area of cost reduction when the frequencies of activities were considered."

We thus end the day and agree that tomorrow we will focus on the organizational process. Each team member will discuss the results of the interviews of the companies he or she investigated regarding the way the companies went about the eleven critical management and organizational processes governing the behavior of their employees. We will report on both the qualitative and quantitative aspects.

TABLE 5. MANN-WHITNEY U-VALUES indicating levels of significance for differences in proportion for two groups across eleven major intervention strategies

INTERVENTION STRATEGY	PROPORTIONS REC	PROPORTIONS DEC	U
BUILDING AN EXECUTIVE TEAM	0.30	0.17	30.5
INTEGRATION	0.12	0.00	13.0
ORGANIZATIONAL DESIGN	0.16	0.17	30.0
PERFORMANCE MANAGEMENT	0.11	0.08	23.0
PHILOSOPHY, CULTURE, VALUES	0.11	0.00	7.0
FINANCIAL DISCIPLINE	0.06	0.04	23.5
COST REDUCTION	0.04	0.05	18.0
PRODUCT-MARKET FOCUS	0.06	0.05	25.5
INCREASING REVENUE	0.01	0.29	7.5
STRATEGIC DEVELOPMENT	0.03	0.04	24.0
RESTRUCTURING AND RATIONALIZING MANUFACTURING or operational processes	0.02	0.08	16.0

TABLE 6. MANN-WHITNEY U-VALUES indicating levels of significance for differences in raw scores for two groups across eleven major intervention strategies

INTERVENTION STRATEGY	RAW SCORES: AVERAGE REC	RAW SCORES: AVERAGE DEC	U
BUILDING AN EXECUTIVE TEAM	11.0	4.2	21.0
INTEGRATION	4.5	0.0	3.0
ORGANIZATIONAL DESIGN	5.2	3.7	25.0
PERFORMANCE MANAGEMENT	5.0	1.0	16.5
PHILOSOPHY, CULTURE, VALUES	3.2	0.0	7.0
FINANCIAL DISCIPLINE	2.0	0.5	20.0
COST REDUCTION	1.2	1.5	22.0
PRODUCT-MARKET FOCUS	2.2	1.2	30.5
INCREASING REVENUE	0.5	4.7	13.0
STRATEGIC DEVELOPMENT	1.0	0.7	29.5
RESTRUCTURING AND RATIONALIZING MANUFACTURING or operational processes	0.5	1.7	17.5

chapter 12

IT IS WEDNESDAY MORNING, and everyone is ready for the day in mission control. During the second phase of our investigation, we focused on the organizational process. Team members will now report on their interviews of the CEOs (in most cases) and/or directors. These interviews followed a structured format that covered the existence of key strategic systems and the process followed to put them in place. Also covered in the interviews were policies and processes vital to the effective functioning of an organization.

As discussed earlier, at the beginning of our mission we developed a structured interview format that included eleven key organizational processes derived from the literature study and the experience of the researcher.

After all interviews were completed, each team member analyzed his or her raw data. At this time, we eliminated issues or aspects that did not differentiate between cases because either all or none of the companies exhibited or manifested a particular issue. What we were looking for were the *differentiating elements* in each process we investigated.

Next, we systematically analyzed the interview protocol for each company in terms of the eleven organizational processes listed earlier. Today we will present our analyses and scoring on a 3-point scale, followed by a discussion of the process and a comparison of cases within each process.

It promises to be a long and fruitful day.

"Well," I say with my best smile, "good morning, all. Are you ready? Each one of you will report first on the findings of your recovered company, then on the findings of your declining companies."

John, as always, is ready to report first on his recovered chemical company. He opens his laptop and starts his PowerPoint presentation, augmenting each slide with information from his notes.

1. Vision and mission (total points = 4). A new vision and mission were not defined through a formal process, but emerged from executive committee meetings. The mission was simply to provide a high quality product in a timely fashion. (Points = 2.)

No formal process was followed to define the mission and vision; the CEO involved his executive team, but no other managers. (Points = 1.)

The mission of the company did not appear in any company documentation, such as a newsletter, could not be accessed by any employee, and was not widely communicated. (Points = 1.)

2. Strategy and direction (total points = 5). The only

strategic planning that took place during the turnaround phase was the development of a formal marketing plan. A comprehensive strategic planning process was introduced four years later, but can unfortunately not be credited to the turnaround phase.

The marketing plan was updated annually and did lead to formalized budgets. This plan indicated current market penetration levels for all segments of the market such as gumboots, sheeting, industrial mouldings, and uncured rubber. On a year-on-year basis, the size of these markets was established, the company's share was determined, competitors' share was determined, and a strategy formulated to increase market share. (Points = 2.)

The CEO and his executive committee mainly developed this marketing plan. The executive team and managers reporting to them went away for a weekend once a year, where the CEO made a four to five hour presentation. This presentation included their achievements during the past year and the strategies they followed to get there, as well as where they should be at the end of the next year and the strategies that they should follow. This presentation was followed by an open debate for approximately one hour. Thereafter, the weekend was enjoyed by the executives and their wives as a gesture of appreciation. (Points = 2.)

The managers received copies of the CEO's slides, but the results of the strategic plan were not widely published and did not contain detailed strategies for every operating unit. (Points = 1.)

3. Environmental scanning (total points = 9). In terms of scanning the external environment, we hired a management-consulting group on a number of occasions to do market

research on behalf of the company. In terms of scanning the internal environment, another group of consultants was brought in to investigate areas of productivity improvement. The executive committee did a SWOT analysis on an annual basis. (Points = 3.)

Environmental scanning was therefore done through formal processes and involved most of the managers in the organization. (Points = 3.)

The environmental scanning resulted in increased productivity and product-market focusing. (Points = 3.)

4. Organizational design (total points = 10). As became apparent from the earlier discussion on structure, major structural changes took place. (Points = 3.)

Major changes also took place in the head count, which was reduced by 200 during the first two years, which represented nearly 25 percent of the total head count. (Points = 3.)

Major changes also took place in the composition of the top executive team with the appointment of a new CEO, a new sales director, and the firing of the general manager of the inland division; this was three changes in a team of five. Other appointments lower down in the organization resulted in more new faces in the management team. (Points = 3.)

The nature of the organizational structure that evolved during the turnaround phase did not deviate significantly from the traditional functional structure. (Points = 1.)

5. Role definition (total points = 6). Top executive roles were formally defined. One of the very first things the new CEO did was to create job descriptions for all his executives. He also required that they write job descriptions for all their subordinate managers. His executives were also required to give him formal organization charts of their departmental

structures. (Points = 3.)

In addition to formal job descriptions, the emphasis in each job was refocused on an annual basis to accommodate current problems and/or issues. All directors had to submit five priority objectives for themselves and for every subordinate manager reporting to them. These priority objectives had to be quantifiable as far as possible. (Points = 3.)

6. Reward systems (total points = 4). Remuneration was based on salary surveys, performance in meeting budgets, and return on assets. (Points = 2.)

Profit bonuses were awarded to managers for exceeding revenue budgets. Based on return on assets, bonuses of up to half their annual salary were awarded to executives. (Points = 2.)

7. Policies and values (total points = 4). No specific set of values was developed except for the one of cooperation. (Points = 1.)

A set of values was therefore not made available to all employees in a documented form. (Points = 1.)

It does not seem that the company became significantly value-driven, yet managers were empowered and were given discretion to make certain decisions. (Points = 2.)

8. Performance management (total points = 9). Performance was certainly managed over a wider base than financial results only. It also included dealing with critical problems, improving productivity, and quality. (Points = 3.)

Activities were primarily controlled through monthly financial results, which were reviewed at the executive committee meetings, and through other systems, such as those described in the next paragraphs. (Points = 3.)

Formal performance management systems and programs

were introduced:

a. Exception reports through the financial pack
b. National Productivity Institute productivity standards
c. Five priority objectives per executive measured on a biannual basis
d. Basis on which salary increments were based
e. Bonus system based on financial results
f. Better Business Bureau of Standards. (Points = 3.)

9. Communication and coordination (total points = 5). At the executive level of the organization, communication and coordination were primarily facilitated through the monthly executive committee meetings and the new development committee meetings. There were other meetings at the middle management level, such as weekly production, monthly sales meetings, etc. This communication structure is not exceptional and is in line with most other companies. There were only two interdepartmental meetings. (Points = 1.)

The CEO met with the directors once a day on an individual basis. He followed an open door policy so that people were able to see him on short notice, and he often cut through formal communication lines to make contact with people who did not directly report to him. Not many opportunities existed for the CEO to meet formally with other staff who reported to his executives, and so he largely left his executives to manage their own staffs. The executive team and other managers met informally on several occasions. (Points = 3.)

The nature of the network was very much intra-departmental; that is, departmental meetings involved only the members of their own departments. (Points = 1.)

10. Decision-making (total points = 7). The new CEO stated that whereas the previous CEO had made all the decisions himself, he (the new CEO) followed a philosophy of management by committee. His executives were empowered and knew how far to go. Because he had a marketing background, he could not involve himself too much in detailed production, distribution, and finance decisions, and he therefore left decision-making in these areas largely to the executives concerned. They were controlled by exception only. The organizational structure was also a decentralized one with few central departments having much control. (Points = 3.)

Although these executives were given some latitude, they did not have authority to hire new people, adjust the salaries of their subordinates, or exceed budgeted expenses. (Points = 1.)

During the turnaround phase, there were few head office or support functions with sufficient power to prescribe restrictive policy to operations. Operations could pursue their objectives without bureaucratic interference from the center. (Points = 3.)

11. Change and transformation (total points = 25). The only opportunity for the new vision of the company to be sold to management and employees was at the annual strategic meeting. (Points = 2.)

Marketing research and other means of external information were used to identify the need for change and new direction. (Points = 3.)

The direction created by the new CEO deviated in terms of becoming an aggressive marketing company with the aim of growing market share from the direction being pursued by the company at the time. (Points = 3.)

The management structure of the organization changed during the three to four year turnaround phase. (Points = 3.)

The company's shares moved from 20 percent to approximately 70 percent during a three-year period. These improvements were achieved not only through aggressive marketing, but also through changes in product quality, product presentation, and market focus. (Points = 3.)

During the turnaround phase, the composition of the management team changed. (Points = 3.)

During the turnaround phase, many new avenues for reducing costs and increasing revenue and profitability were explored and implemented. Much of this was achieved through the bonus incentive scheme, a profit improvement program, and the new development committee. (Points = 3.)

Policies and values did not dramatically change. (Points = 2.)

At this point, having given the primary data, John pauses, takes a sip of water, and begins to walk around the room.

"If we summarize the intervention strategies of this recovered company, we find the following," he says. "The company developed a strategic marketing plan that included market segmentation, market share per segment, and competitor activities. This plan showed where the company had low market share and at the same time, high surplus capacity.

"The CEO became personally involved in marketing the company and selling its products, especially taking responsibility for negotiating with the top fifty customers. Cost-saving measures included reducing head count, elevating asset control and management to a more professional level (which resulted in reduction in stock levels), reducing debtor days, and freezing salaries for the first two years. Among management changes he made, he appointed a quality control executive to assist with low quality problems and upgrade delivered quality to customers. He also appointed a human resources executive to assist with the growing complexities of industrial relations, trade union negotiations, and productivity and motivation. He forced the operational director and sales director, whose disagreements resulted in open animosity between them and their departments, to either resign or sort out their differences. He introduced incentive scheme with gross profit margins set as targets. When the budgeted target was achieved, bonus was awarded to those who achieved their target equal to the fourteenth check, with an incremental sliding scale up to a sixteenth check. He appointed a new sales director to increase service levels and improve relationships with existing customers.

"The CEO asked the general manager for the inland division to leave, and through restructuring scrapped the position of inland general manager. The two managers who reported to him were made to report to the works director and sales director. He appointed a technical manager to improve quality through product and process engineering, targeted major customers in the market segments indicated by the strategic marketing plan, and sent the sales team out to gain their business. He developed a mission statement.

"When the CEO learned that twenty-five sophisticated injection moulding machines were being underutilized, the executive team adopted a strategy of filling capacity at a marginal cost to recover overheads. High volumes were thus achieved and profit margins gradually increased over a two-year period to 25 percent. He adopted a business philosophy of moving away from low-quality products, indifferent service, and political in fighting to high quality products, careful customer service, and cooperation among departments.

"To control activities in all areas where costs could be saved, he introduced a system of exception reporting, set clear performance standards for all key activities of the business, and identified areas where productivity could be improved, costs saved, and profits improved. To set standards for manufacturing performance, he introduced the Better Business Bureau of Standards Quality System. He formed a development committee under the chairmanship of the marketing director to evaluate and structure all new developments, such as processes and products.

"The CEO introduced a new profit improvement plan and motivated his staff to identify areas where greater profits could be achieved. He chaired numerous other meetings at lower levels to facilitate integration and coordination. He appointed a marketing service manager and a production services manager and created a Friday afternoon meeting where all managers got together to bounce ideas off each other and update themselves on the latest developments. He established close and solid relationships with the company's top twenty-five suppliers to assist in obtaining good quality products at the lowest prices."

Drawing our attention to his PowerPoint presentation again, John shows us a list headed "Problems Being Experienced When New CEO Took Over":

a. Preparation by previous CEO for expansion in sales that never materialized. This resulted in expensive overhead costs.

b. No strategic leadership by previous CEO.
c. No formal marketing strategy. Sales plummeted.
d. No adequate cost control systems existed. There were huge raw material variances.
e. Company was overstaffed.
f. Unacceptable customer service. The company was losing key accounts.
g. Company suffered bad image and name in the market place due to bad quality.

"No assets were sold," John concludes, "and the recovered company is operating under what is essentially the same executive team, except for the new CEO. One dismissal and a few new appointments achieved the turnaround, and no strategic planning process was introduced."

After we have all commended John for his fine work, it is now Carin's turn to report on her recovered pharmaceutical company. She opens her laptop and switches it on. This draws our attention to her PowerPoint presentation. Like John, she comments on the slides where more information is needed.

1. Vision and mission (total points = 9). Mission and vision statements were developed and documented for the group as a whole and for each of its operating companies. (Points = 3.)

A formal process was followed in developing a mission statement, the vision, and a set of values. Although one operating company succeeded well using a participative method, the others' initial attempts were superficial. They managed to succeed the third time around. (Points = 3.)

The mission and vision formulated in this way were properly documented and were therefore widely communicated and accepted. Mission and vision were written in hiring brochures and other documentation. (Points = 3.)

2. Strategy and direction (total points = 10). As they were doing the SWOT analysis, each of the operating companies developed an annual strategic plan by business unit from the inside out and from the outside in. Financial computer models were used to determine "what is" and the effects of different strategies on return on managed assets. These strategies were separately presented to the CEO, who then made his own contributions. This was followed by a formal presentation by each company to the group's executive team, from which a group strategy was developed. These strategies were then presented to the board. Budgets were developed from these strategic plans and operating results were monitored against these budgets. (Points = 4.)

This process involved the top executive team of all operating companies in the group. Three to four days per year were allocated for the strategic planning, during which the executives met away from the office and out of town. (Points = 3.)

This strategic planning process resulted in a published strategic plan containing detailed strategies for each operating unit. The plan was made available to all managers in the operating companies. (Points = 3.)

3. Environmental scanning (total points = 9). Great effort was spent to ensure adequate scanning of the external environment and updating of managerial thought in the group. This involved conducting the SWOT analysis during the annual strategic planning meeting, constant overseas travel by executives to study the best concepts and ideas in the world, and continuous presentations by outside directors, consultants, and visiting speakers. (Points = 3.)

All of this was made into formal processes involving a large number of managers. (Points = 3.)

This information was used to change the culture of the group for product-market refocusing and strategic planning. (Points = 3.)

4. Organizational design (total points = 12). The organizational structure of the group changed significantly during the turnaround phase with the subtraction of human resources, public relations, social responsibility; and public relations; the sale of a manufacturing concern; and the change of finance and property into profit centers. (Points = 3.)

The head count of the group grew by about 1,000 to 4,500 during the turnaround phase. (Points = 3.)

Major changes took place in the composition of the top management team during the turnaround phase. (Points = 3.)

In terms of the nature of the restructuring, there was an initial shift from dependence to independence and, later, a move toward interdependence. The structure shifted from a pure functional/hierarchical one to a decentralized federal structure, supplemented by concepts derived from a team structure. This team structure was composed of the board, the M.D. Forum, a group computer committee working on problem issues of the medical industry, a committee working on group benefits, a project team working on optimizing office accommodations, and a project team working on information technology. (Points = 3.)

5. Role definition (total points = 6). The CEO did not believe in job descriptions. The approach he followed was the concept of a "covenant," whereby he detailed to his executives what their assets were, what outputs were expected outputs,

and the rules and values according to which they should operate. (Points = 3.)

A study of the intervention strategies during this turnaround situation made it clear that the definitions of roles of executives, annual emphasis, and objectives set all flowed from the annual strategic planning process, the business philosophy, and values the CEO advocated. (Points = 3.)

6. Reward system (total points = 5). Remuneration was based on job grade, which is an accepted norm. Added to this were the performance bonus and share participation scheme, which rewarded people not purely on seniority but also in terms of contribution. (Points = 2.)

The remuneration policy was extremely creative, in that at senior levels it was based on the concept of a covenant whereby executives could state what they needed in order to meet performance standards. Included here were not only financial issues, but also personal needs. In addition to this, employees could start managing their own capital share of the retirement fund. In this way the responsibility for the retirement fund shifted from the company to the employees. Every employee could, at any point, examine his/her fund account, see how it had grown, and decide to put in a greater contribution or draw off their fund account. A wide choice of health insurance options also existed. (Points = 3.)

7. Policies and values (total points = 8). All three operating divisions of the group were required to develop mission and vision statements and a set of values according to which people could operate. The concept of the covenant with executives added to a value culture; executives were asked what they needed to self-actualize. Initially, the needs were material, but in time they shifted to other matters. Policies were reduced

and trimmed to make way for a more value-driven culture. (Points = 3.)

A set of values was formally documented and made available to all staff members. It also formed the basis for negotiations with the trade unions. (Points = 3.)

A "road show" was held and attended by group CEOs and directors. This is where the values were announced. Although much was done, the CEOs felt that the organization was not yet truly value-driven. However, trimming down and rationalizing policies significantly increased the discretionary powers of managers with regard to matters such as staffing, strategies, and structures. (Points = 2.)

8. Performance management (total points = 9). Performance was managed and controlled through the monthly financial results and through meetings on qualitative and quantitative issues. The CEO used a performance and development discussion to manage long-term performance. He believed that the performance of a senior executive was more than just the review of certain key objectives and to an extent compared with a covenant between him and his executives. As far as possible, the responsibility for performance and performance improvement was moved to the employee, who had to decide how he or she could develop his or her performance. (Points = 3.)

Performance was managed over a wide base, covering not only financial issues but also aspects such as people development, building structures and teams, and innovation. (Points = 3.)

Performance and development discussions occurred on a regular basis (more than once a year for all top executives) and could be considered as a performance management system.

(Points = 3.)

9. Communication and coordination (total points = 7). A formal network of meetings and project teams was created to facilitate communication and coordination. Between three and seven such meetings were instituted. (Points = 2.)

These meetings, committees, and projects were inter-disciplinary. Their purpose was to coordinate efforts on special issues and formulate policy. Most of the meetings in the network structure involved members from various departments who had a wide skills base. (Points = 3.)

The CEO met formally once a month with every executive reporting to him. There were also many opportunities for the CEO to meet with staff other than his direct reporters. He maintained that there were no sensitivities where managers below his direct reporters came directly to him to discuss a problem – if the problem had to be resolved at his level, he said, then people had to understand that it had to be done. Though he often met with his managers and their teams, the top executive team of the group seldom met on a formal basis; meetings were scheduled on an ad hoc basis. At the time of data collection vertical communication seemed to be more powerful than horizontal communication. (Points = 2.)

10. Decision-making (total points = 9). The group's decision-making power was sufficiently decentralized, as evidenced by the following two examples. First, the CEO of one of the operating companies bought another company. Having the requisite authority to do this, he did not have to consult or get the permission of the group CEO. Second, one of the operating companies bought an information system, also without the necessity for consultation with the group CEO. (Points = 3.)

Executives and managers were empowered and had a large degree of discretion in terms of key decisions, such as hiring of staff, salary adjustments, expenditure, and granting credit. (Points = 3.)

As a result, the restructuring moved away from the traditional concept of strong head offices, which prescribe to the operational divisions in terms of policy, to diverting the decision-making power back into the operating companies. Restrictive policies were reduced and values were introduced to lead to greater discretion in managerial decision-making. (Points = 3.)

11. Change and transformation (total points = 26). Many opportunities were created and used to sell the new vision of the group to relevant staff members. (Points = 3.)

Significant external information and processes were used to identify the group's need for change and a new direction. (Points = 3.)

The new direction of the company deviated materially from where it stood before the turnaround phase. (Points = 3.)

During the turnaround phase, the structure of the organization changed significantly. (Points = 3.)

During this phase, the product-market focus of the various operating companies received much attention and they became more focused. (Points = 3.)

The composition of the executive management team changed dramatically during the turnaround phase. (Points = 3.)

The pricing structure of the various operating companies also changed significantly. (Points = 3.)

During the turnaround phase, some avenues for increasing

revenue were explored and implemented. (Points = 2.)

Policies and values have also changed, with the values program receiving significant attention. (Points = 3.)

"If we summarize the intervention strategies of this recovered company," Carin says as she sits down, "we find the following. The new CEO had to refocus the attitudes of his top executive team away from a strictly analytical attitude and toward a more marketing and innovating attitude. He developed and widely communicated key values to support the issues and introduced a management philosophy according to which executives could manage their businesses.

"In one of the operating divisions of this group, a new CEO, merchandising director, human resources director, marketing director, operations director and all regional managers were all replaced. In the second operating division of this group, new appointments were also made as new marketing, financial, and merchandising directors came on board. The operations director was transferred to another division, and another manager was promoted to this position. The human resource manager was removed. In the third and fourth operating divisions, all of the second line managers were replaced by appointments from outside.

"To change the culture, the new CEO spent much time advocating three specific models that indicate socio-economic megatrends. The first was a stakeholder model reflecting stakeholders' changing perceptions; the second, a model illustrating the ethnic and demographic spread of leadership; and the third, a megatrends seminar where fifteen speakers sketched a Rip van Winkle scenario for the U.S. market. As each operating division was differentiated from the other operating companies in the group and from its competitors, marketing, financial, human resources, merchandising, and operations strategies had to be changed to focus on these opportunities. The CEO introduced an incentive scheme to pitch rewards where efforts had to be made and developed and introduced share participation scheme. He also reviewed the reward system and made it more flexible, offering executives a buffet of perks to choose from.

"Restructuring the group itself, the CEO reduced the head office and decentralized key functions. The group's human resources, social responsibility, benefits, and public relations departments were disbanded, decentralized, and turned into operating companies where they could add more value. He transformed the finance department into a financial services division, which became a profit center, put all property issues into a property company, which also became a profit center, and sold off any company that had no synergy with the existing core business."

Carin stands up and walks over to her PowerPpoint presentation and switches it on again. "I want to mention some general notes of interest," she says, and she reads her list of problems the new CEO experienced on appointment:

a. Strong centralized head office dominating the operations and taking away shopping flair and innovation.
b. Management team insensitive to new and changing socio-economic environment.
c. The group insufficiently differentiated from its competitors

Carin switches off her laptop and returns to her seat. After a short break during which I notice the team members talking in the hall about Carin's report, I nod to Tim and gesture to him to begin. He opens his laptop and starts his presentation on his recovered retail company.

1. Vision and mission (total points = 9). The vision and mission of the company were clearly defined through its shared values. A formal process was followed to define the vision and mission. Most managers were involved in the shared value program, which was repeated a few years later. (Points = 3.)

The mission of the organization and its values appeared in numerous company documents and were frequently emphasized. The vision and mission were therefore accessible to all employees. (Points = 3.)

2. Strategy and direction (total points = 9). A formal, annual strategic planning process with specific stages existed and resulted in the budget plan for the following year. This process called for future group meetings every second month, a strategic meeting involving all directors for two to three days every six months, and an annual executive conference with all middle managers. (Points = 3.)

The CEO, his directors, and all middle managers were involved in this process. A number of days were spent on the development of strategy. (Points = 3.)

The result of the strategic planning process was not only a published budget and a plan for the next year, but also the creation of project teams to investigate and address key problem issues. These plans were available to all managers and were presented to them twice a year. (Points = 3.)

3. Environmental scanning (total points = 10). Specific processes and projects existed to scan environmental changes:

a. Annual tracking study to measure the company's progress against competitors
b. Quarterly mystery shopper study
c. Quarterly price-pointing study
d. Monthly customer service level measurement
e. Fortnightly competitive shop-outs
f. Salary surveys
g. Other ad hoc research. (Points = 4.)

These were formal processes and not ad hoc events and thus involved large numbers of managers. (Points = 3.)

The environmental scanning covered not only the external environment, but there was also considerable emphasis on the scanning of the internal environment through three SWOT analyses – one on competitors, one on staff, and one on productivity. These were used to strategize and determine new objectives and plans. (Points = 3.)

4. Organizational design (total points = 8). Moderate structural changes were made during the recovery phase. Two specialist positions were created, one for industrial relations, the other for sales promotions. For better control, a new layer of management – the general manager – was introduced. (Points = 2.)

Some changes in head count took place. (Points = 2.)

The composition of the top executive team changed drastically. This was largely as a result of promotions from within. (Points = 2.)

The nature of the structure moved from a traditional functional structure to one that incorporated elements of a decentralized federal structure. (Points = 2.)

5. Role definition (total points = 6). Top executive roles

were defined by formal written job descriptions with specific objectives and targets for every executive. (Points = 3.)

The roles of top executives were refocused on an annual basis through specific objectives and targets to be achieved in the following financial year. These objectives and targets flowed naturally from the strategic planning process. (Points = 3.)

6. Reward systems (total points = 4). Remuneration was based on a grading system as well as on performance in defined financial areas. The grading system was adjusted twice a year. (Points = 2.)

Although remuneration was not flexible, there were numerous bonuses in addition to normal salary, pension, and medical benefits. (Points = 2.)

7. Policies and values (total points = 8). A set of well-defined values existed through the shared values program. (Points = 3.)

A specific shared values program was undertaken. The values were available to all staff and appeared frequently in company documentation. (Points = 3.)

Although some empowerment existed where managers could use their own discretion in decision-making, policies were perhaps still too restrictive. In addition to the set of values, training manuals existed for every job, including policies and procedures according to which jobs are performed. These may be a little too prescriptive. (Points = 2.)

8. Performance management (total points = 8). Activities were controlled by the monthly financial results and review meetings on financial results and operations. While a network of meetings, project teams, and committees also existed through which activities were controlled, these were not as

extensive as in other cases studied. (Points = 2.)

Performance was managed over a wide base, including financial results, values, and service levels. (Points = 3.)

A formal performance management system consisting of performance appraisals and bonus systems existed. Performance was monitored on a monthly, quarterly, six-monthly, and annual basis, depending on the issue to be measured. (Points = 3.)

9. Communication and coordination (total points = 7). A formal network of meetings existed through which information was communicated and activities coordinated. There were three to five interdepartmental meetings, most of them within departments. Monthly operations meetings took place in which key staff members from all departments were integrated. In addition, there were future group meetings, focus groups, status meetings, and various other project team meetings. (Points = 2.)

Communication was still largely of an intradepartmental nature, with not enough interdisciplinary integration. (Points = 2.)

The CEO met formally and individually on a monthly basis with each executive and followed an open door policy, with staff being able to see him at short notice. The CEO also met regularly with other staff members during store visits and made additional contact with them by attending divisional meetings. (Points = 3.)

10. Decision-making (total points = 4). Although decentralization of decision-making power had taken place during the recovery phase, the structure was still fairly centralized. (Points = 2.)

Executives and managers were empowered, but at the time

of the study they did not yet have the authority to appoint their own staff, terminate the services of a subordinate, adjust their salaries, or exceed budgeted expenditure. (Points = 1.)

Strong head office departments prescribed to the operating divisions, thereby limiting their powers and latitude in decision-making. (Points = 1.)

11. Change and transformation (total points = 18). There were some opportunities for the mission and vision of the company to be sold to staff members, for example, the shared values program, but more could be done in this area. (Points = 2.)

Market research projects were constantly undertaken to gather information to identify the need for change and new direction. (Points = 3.)

Because this company was well positioned within its market sector, the direction defined during the recovery phase deviated only moderately from its previous position. (Points = 2.)

Structures have not changed materially. (Points = 2.)

Products, product presentation, and market focus changed very little. (Points = 1.)

There were some changes to the composition of the management team, but these where more a result of natural career progression than bringing management in from outside to achieve a change in philosophy and culture. (Points = 2.)

The pricing structure of the company changed to some extent. (Points = 2.)

Few new avenues for increasing revenue, other than the traditional business, were explored and implemented. (Points = 1.)

The policies and values of the organization changed

materially. (Points = 3.)

"If we summarize the intervention strategies of this recovered retail company," Tim says, "we find the following. They established the value of teamwork; no matter where the problem was, the team was responsible for it. They introduced an incentive scheme and made new division director appointments in human resources, finance, and operations. They implemented a shared values program and clarified executive responsibilities, giving executives decision-making powers to use at their own discretion.

"The new CEO became personally involved in the marketing activities of the company. He personally negotiated with the advertising agency and took co-responsibility for this function. He conducted climate studies to measure the results of the shared values program and monitor the culture of the organization. He created "praise" committees in every branch and cost center to monitor the extent to which behavior met values. He developed a performance measurement program and introduced a bonus system with a different theme each year. He also introduced awards for performance in addition to the incentive scheme and the bonus system.

"The new CEO installed an answering machine at his home and gave the telephone number to all staff members, thus encouraging them to phone and records all incidents of behavior that did not meet the values of the company. He personally responded to these messages, He changed the operational structure, reducing the number of branches reporting to a regional controller, and created more specialist functions at the regional level to expand and strengthen the sales and credit functions. He created a "future group," which was an inter-disciplinary committee with the aim of developing strategies focusing on the long-term issues of the business. He reduced head count, reduced the vehicle fleet by 10 percent, and implemented training programs for all jobs."

Tim concludes his presentation with some general notes on problems the new CEO experienced on appointment:

a. The executive team did not work well together.
b. Cost growth outstripped sales growth.
c. Cash consumption was unacceptable.
d. Profit margins were too low.
e. Return on assets was too low.

As Tim concludes and sits down at the table, Scott jumps to his feet before I even give him his cue. Rather eager, that boy, I think to myself. I must keep an eye on him. He will be valuable to the company in the future.

"Here is my report on the recovered freight company," Scott announces, beginning his presentation.

1. Vision and mission (total points = 9). The mission of the group was clearly defined. (Points = 3.)

This definition was done through a formal organizational development program that involved a large number of managers over and above the CEO and directors. (Points = 3.)

The mission statement appeared in all strategic plans, sales documentation, and other company literature. (Points = 3.)

2. Strategy and direction (total points = 9). A formal annual strategic planning process was followed. It comprised several stages and led to a final budget. This was a bottom-up process, where various operating units prepared plans and budgets within broad parameters. These were presented at the meeting and, on acceptance, a presentation was made to the

group for final approval. Three to four days away from the office were spent on this annually. (Points = 3.)

This process involved the CEO, directors, and the next two levels of management. (Points = 3.)

The strategic plan was then broken down further into divisional and departmental plans. (Points = 3.)

3. Environmental scanning (total Points = 9). Managers pooled their information about and experiences with the market during the annual strategic planning meeting. In addition to this, external consultants undertook two major market research surveys on the freight and transportation market and on customer perceptions. (Points = 3.)

This scanning was a formal process, rather than an ad hoc event. (Points = 3.)

This information was used to restrategize for the next financial year. It was also used to develop new products and scale down products and services indicated to be in decline. (Points = 3.)

4. Organizational design (total Points = 12). Intervention strategies were used to make major changes to the structure. (Points = 3.)

Head count was reduced. (Points = 3.)

Six of the seven top executive positions were changed. Two positions were refocused with the same incumbents and the other four with new appointments. (Points = 3.)

The structure was moved away from a purely functional/ hierarchical form to one that incorporated strong elements of a network or cluster organization. (Points = 3.)

5. Role definition (total points = 6). The top executive team was given specific job descriptions, mandates, and objectives to achieve. (Points = 3.)

These flowed from a very elaborate and comprehensive strategic planning process that was adjusted annually to mark changes in the environment and new challenges. (Points = 3.)

6. Reward systems (total points = 4). Remuneration was based on a job-grading system, salary surveys, and year-to-year profit growth. (Points = 2.)

In addition to basic salary, normal fringe benefits, a company car, and a bonus check, executives also shared in the gross annual profit. (Points = 2.)

7. Policies and values (total points = 8). A values program was undertaken and involved a large proportion of the managers in the company. (Points = 3.)

A video expressing these values was created and shown to all existing employees and incorporated into an induction program for new employees. The values were also printed on large posters, which were displayed in passages and boardrooms. (Points = 3.)

Although this organization was moving away from a policy driven culture toward a more empowering culture, policies still restricted operational decision-making. (Points = 2.)

8. Performance management (total points = 7). Initially, performance management was largely based on financial issues, but the focus has now changed to include management development, customer relations, market share gain, and other non-financial issues. (Points = 3.)

Performance was controlled through the financial results and a network of committees and task forces on strategic issues. One-on-one discussions with executives took place, but had not been formalized into an appraisal system. (Points = 2.)

Performance appraisals were introduced, but were not frequently implemented at the top end. (Points = 2.)

9. Communications and coordination (total points = 9). An extensive network structure of meetings and committees was created. It had sixteen interdepartmental and interdisciplinary task forces and committees, involving not only staff members from other departments or divisions or regions, but also outside consultants. (Points = 3.)

The distinct aim of the network structure was to create integration and interdisciplinary focus on key corporate problems and strategic issues. (Points = 3.)

The CEO met regularly with his executives and undertook visits to the various operations on a monthly basis. (Points = 3.)

10. Decision-making (total points = 9). Even before the turnaround phase, the company was decentralized. The new CEO extended this by further decentralizing the manpower, marketing, and sales functions into regions. All that remained at the center was corporate finance. Much of the finance department had been decentralized on a previous occasion. (Points = 3.)

Executives in the regions had total discretion in the appointment of staff, salary adjustments, credit terms, and so forth. (Points = 3.)

Thanks to the decentralization of central functions, no head office departments existed to prescribe to or limit decision-making in the operating divisions. (Points = 3.)

11. Change and transformation (total points = 24). The CEO visited each region at least four times in the first year to sell the new vision. (Points = 3.)

Organizational development processes were used to teach managers and staff the need to change. (Points = 3.)

When the company gained new focus, the new direction of

the business deviated materially from the previous direction. (Points = 3.)

Structures changed materially. (Points = 3.)

Products, product presentation and product-market focus changed to a lesser extent. (Points = 2.)

When the company's intervention strategies were discussed, the composition of the management team began to change. (Points = 3.)

Pricing policy was clarified rather than changed. (Points = 2.)

Many new avenues for increasing revenue were explored. (Points = 3.)

Values were established and some policies were changed. (Points = 2.)

"If we summarize the intervention strategies of this recovered freight company," Scott says, "we find the following. A team building exercise was undertaken to bring together a widely dispersed and hostile team. Changes included product-market refocus, a redefinition of the role of the head office, and decentralization of the human resource function. Finance was strengthened by the appointment of more high-powered chartered accountants at the head office and in the regions. A computer executive and a business development manager were appointed at the head office. One of the regional executives was transferred to a 'specialist ships agency' position, and the marketing division was decentralized when the marketing director was transferred to another region.

"The company brought the logistics division, part of another group company to the head office and sold off transport operations owned in another country. Because transport is critical, they formed a trans-border division to specialize in transport booking and take advantage of buying power. They disinvested in three other countries by transferring one operation to another group company, selling shares in a cold storage company to strengthen the balance sheet in another country and improve gearing, and paying a dividend to shareholders for the first time in six years. Twenty staff homes were sold to generate cash and improve gearing, and the wholesale tourist division in the northern region was also sold, along with two cargo vessels. The company separated activities in Europe, keeping traditional freight management activities, but moving trading and vessel activities to another group company. A smaller competitor was purchased.

"The board was restructured and an executive committee consisting of top executives formed to meet quarterly. The CEO introduced planning from the bottom up, rather than from top down, thus giving managers the opportunity to get involved in the planning process. He created a network of five project teams to set strategic initiatives into action and formulate a new mission statement. Working capital management, including credit control, was improved, and all financial systems were computerized and decentralized."

Finally, like the others, Scott lists some problems the new CEO experienced on appointment:

a. Company not focused
b. Large, cumbersome board of directors, including executives
c. Traditional freight activities running at losses
d. No stable management team
e. Low levels of profitability in all regions and countries

f. Company not well understood by larger group.
    Relationships with other group companies were
    not good.

At this, Scott concludes and sits down.

I stand up and stifle a yawn. "This has been another long day, team," I say. "We will continue tomorrow morning, when you will give feedback on the results of your declining companies in the same format as we did on the recovered companies. Have a wonderful evening."

chapter 13

IT IS THURSDAY MORNING and Tim is not in mission control.

"Where is he?" I ask. "It's not like him to be late."

"I didn't see his car in the parking garage," Carin says, "and I assume I'm the last one in this morning." She pauses and gives a wicked smile. "Well," she adds, "other than you, Adam."

Twenty-five minutes later, Tim finally arrives. "Sorry I'm late," he apologizes, setting his laptop on the conference table and taking off his jacket and rolling up his sleeves. "We all overslept, and that meant it was a rush to get the children and myself ready so I could get them to school on time."

As Tim takes his seat, John stands up, opens his laptop, and starts his PowerPoint presentation report on his declining chemical company.

---

1. Vision and mission (total points = 4). The CEO stated that he did not believe in mission statements. They had a general vision and direction, he said, but it was not formally defined or published. (Points = 2.)

The company followed no process to develop this general vision. It was forged in deliberations between the CEO and the chairman, with one or two other executives involved from time to time. (Points = 1.)

No vision statement existed in writing. (Points = 1.)

2. Strategy and direction (total points = 7). Little time was spent informally on defining a long-term vision. However, the only evidence of a strategic plan was the budget. Department heads had to draw up their budgets within an overall specified framework. (Points = 2.)

The budget process did not include total strategy. Only the CEO and directors participated, with the next line of managers making budget presentations and setting objectives. (Points = 2.)

Departmental and divisional managers developed detailed production, sales, and cost budgets. (Points = 3.)

3. Environmental scanning (total points = 3). Ad hoc experiences of the management team served the purpose of any formal scanning of the environment. No objective, valid, external information was gathered through other means. (Points = 1.)

No environmental scanning process existed. (Points = 1.)

Ad hoc experiences and information were used, but due to there being no scanning process or strategic planning process, their use was questionable. (Points = 1.)

4. Organizational design (total points = 9). The company's structure changed from an operating structure to a group

structure, with the creation of new positions and the recruiting of new talent from outside the organization. (Points = 2.)

Head count reduction of 20-25 percent took place over a four-year period. (Points = 3.)

Four new appointments from outside were made to the top executive team of eleven executives. Another few internal promotions were also made. (Points = 2.)

The structure changed from being a purely functional structure to one that incorporated elements of federal decentralization. It had not yet succeeded, however, in completely achieving a total transformation to a federal decentralized structure. (Points = 2.)

5. Role definition (total points = 3). No job description existed for any manager in this organization. They operated according to a set of objectives with no clear indication of results. (Points = 2.)

Because hardly any strategic planning processes existed, the company's objectives were ad hoc and to some extent prescribed by the CEO. (Points = 1.)

6. Reward systems (total points = 4). Neither grading nor salary survey were used. Performance evaluations were gathered from applicants for positions and recruitment agencies. (Points = 1.)

A flexible remuneration system was developed with a cafeteria-style shopping list of benefits. A shared participation scheme and profit sharing, resulting in a bonus salary check, had been introduced. (Points = 3.)

7. Values and policies (total points = 4). No formal set of values existed. No documentation could be provided. The CEO maintained that the company put its values across in a subtle way, but without referring to a set of values.

(Points = 1.)

No set of values was formally made available to staff. (Points = 1.)

Although no set of values existed, because of its decentralized nature, the company, allowed some measure of discretion and empowerment. (Points = 2.)

8. Performance management (total points = 4). Performance management was largely based on financial and production, but there was no emphasis on people development, customer relations, marketing, team building, and so forth. (Points = 1.)

Financial results served as the basis for measuring performance. Little else existed over and above this objective. (Points = 1.)

In some departments, performance appraisal systems existed, but the CEO did not require executives to implement them. (Points = 2.)

9. Communication and coordination (total points = 3). The company had a network of seven meetings, but only two of these were interdepartmental and interdisciplinary. (Points = 1.)

The nature of the meeting structure perpetuated the company's segmented, hierarchical culture. There was no integrative, horizontal culture. (Points = 1.)

The CEO met with all of his executives on a one-on-one basis, but few other opportunities were created for internal contact or contact with staff lower down in the structure. (Points = 1.)

10. Decision-making (total points = 6). Some decentralization had taken place, but central control and prescription were still evident in the form of powerful central

departments and corporate policies. (Points = 2.)

Executives and managers had some, but not yet total, discretion in decisions with financial implications, such as appointment of staff, salary adjustments, credit terms, and leases and rentals. (Points = 2.)

A conscious effort had been made by management to reduce the influence of centralized departments that prescribed to operations. (Points = 2.)

11. Change and transformation (total points = 17). Some opportunities were created to sell the company's vision, but these opportunities were not in line with other cases studied. (Points = 1.)

No market research was done in the company and no other external sources of information were used to motivate transformation and change. (Points = 1.)

The current direction of the company differed from the old direction in that some new markets had been penetrated. (Points = 2.)

The company's structure had changed to some extent, in that new business units had been created to enter new markets. (Points = 2.)

Market focus, products, and product presentation had also changed to some extent. (Points = 2.)

The composition of the management team had also changed to some extent. (Points = 2.)

The pricing structure had hardly changed. (Points = 3.)

Many new avenues for increasing revenue were explored, and diversification into other markets where the same basic chemicals could be used was successfully achieved. (Points = 3.)

Policies and particularly values had not changed at all.

(Points = 1.).

Here John sits down, turns off his laptop, and says, "Let me summarize this declining company's intervention strategies. We find the following. Tactical moves in pricing policy and structure made it difficult for competitors to determine the company's prices to clients. The company changed its pricing policy. Based on trust relations with its clients, it obtained orders and delivered chemicals, and at the end of the season finalized prices based on micro- and macro-market conditions. They managed to get better prices this way. The company expanded its market activities to specific regions through the appointment of two sales people to sell their products. Volumes increased by 20 percent as a result.

"The company also started exporting, bought a share for $4 million in a chemical plant, and achieved control over the supply of a base chemical in the manufacture of fertilizers. This led to an overcapacity of nitrogen. Nitrogen reserves not used in fertilizer were used to enter other markets.

"The company also formed a new company allied to the fertilizer industry to specialize in cultivating seed for the agricultural industry. The company created a new trading company to handle fertilizer, maize, and seed exports to Europe. To expand the seed operation, it acquired the seed cultivating company of another large industrial concern and the local subsidiary of a European firm and consolidated these into its own seed operation to establish it as one of the largest seed suppliers in the U.S. The company doubled the production capacity of one of the plants and undertook productivity studies to improve plant utilization. It also introduced technological improvements. It reduced fertilizer plant staff levels by 48 percent and placed greater emphasis on achieving a greater percentage of sales through agricultural co-ops."

As John is finishing, Linda opens the door ever so slightly and pokes her head through. "Adam," she whispers, "do you want me to bring in the refreshments now or later?"

"Now!" everyone choruses, and she wheels in a cart of bottled water and some pastries. Scott goes over to help her. "Thank you, Linda," I say. "Scott, while you're there, you may pass us each some refreshments." Then I turn to Carin and tell her that she can begin her report.

Carin's report is on her declining pharmaceutical company. She opens her Power Point presentation.

1. Vision and mission (total points = 5). The mission of the company was clearly defined by the CEO. (Points = 3.)

No formal process was followed, however. The mission was mainly developed by the CEO, with ad hoc input from some of the executives. (Points = 1.)

The vision and mission of the company were not widely communicated. They did not appear in company documentation. Literature could not be accessed by employees. Vision and mission were, however, contained in the budget presentation to the holding company. (Points = 1.)

2. Strategy and direction (total points = 5). In January of every year, the directors spent three days developing an operations strategy. However, this involved only operations planning and did not result in an overall corporate strategic plan. (Points = 2.)

This process involved only the top management team and was not a cross-section of all levels of management. The top management team spent three (or four) days per year away from the office in conference. (Points = 2.)

The result of this operations planning session was a published plan containing action plans, responsibilities, and deadlines. The operations plan was, however, available only to directors. (Points = 1.)

3. Environmental scanning (total points = 6). During the annual three-day operations planning session, scanning of the environment took place through presentations made to the directors by an economist, political observers, and suppliers. A competitor analysis was also done, and the results of numerous market research projects were considered. (Points = 3.)

In addition to the market research, a semi-formal planning process was followed, but not all managers were involved. (Points = 1.)

The information gained at the off-site meeting was used during the operations planning session, but it was not incorporated into a corporate strategic plan. (Points = 2.)

4. Organizational design (total points = 4). Despite any changes, the company's organizational structure remained fairly stable over the period of review. There were no major additions or subtractions of functions, no changes to a different organization design. (Points = 1.)

The number of employees, as reflected by the head count year-on-year, reflected no drastic changes, except through natural growth. (Points = 1.)

The composition of the top management team did not change. Most of the current executives had been with the organization for many years. (Points = 1.)

The company was characterized by a traditional functional, or hierarchical, structure. The company did not avail itself of other design options. (Points = 1.)

5. Role definition (total points = 5). Although employees

at lower levels in the organization had job descriptions, role definitions for executives were not documented. (Points = 2.)

A "game plan" was documented as a result of the off-site operational planning session. It incorporated a slight change in direction in the market. From this game plan, specific objectives were derived for every operational and support unit. The game plan was submitted to the group board; when the board approved it, company executives began to implement it. (Points = 3.)

6. Reward system (total points = 3). For about 400 staff members, from a total employee base of 1,225, remuneration varied on a monthly basis, based on substantial commissions and bonuses earned. (All sales staff was on a commission basis, whereas general managers, buyers, merchandising managers, and departmental managers received bonuses based on the bottom line of every store according to a set formula.) For salaried staff, remuneration was based on a job-grading system. For lower levels, it was negotiated with the union. For these job categories, remuneration was largely based on contribution. (Points = 2.)

Aside from the creative commission and bonus system, all other employees were remunerated on a very traditional basis of salary plus a bonus check. For senior executives, no specific remuneration system existed. (Points = 1.)

7. Policies and values (total points = 4). A list of six values existed and was signed by all employees and every new employee during his or her induction training program. These values were developed not through a specific process but by only the CEO and the human resources director. (Points = 2.)

These six values did not often appear in company

literature and were not often referred to during meetings and presentations. They were not available to employees on a continuous basis. They were discussed only during the hiring process. (Points = 1.)

The company was not yet value-driven. It was rule-driven. Managers at the operating level had very little discretionary power in decision-making and largely acted within the company's policies and procedures. Policies were updated on a regular basis, but were quite prescriptive, leaving little discretion for decision-making. (Points = 1.)

8. Performance management (total points = 3.) Performance was mostly managed through the monthly financial results and without a more comprehensive assessment of management performance on the basis of people development, building structures and teams, client relations, and innovation. The performance management system thus consisted mainly of the financial pack (budgets, profit, and lost accounts), with some informal discussions with store managers on their point-of-sale (POS) analysis by head office executives during monthly visits. (Points = 1.)

Activities were controlled only through monthly financial results, and POS analysis. Regional managers met with every area manager on a monthly basis to review their profit and loss sheets and POS accounts. No network of meetings, project teams, or committees existed through which initiatives beyond finances were controlled. (Points = 1.)

No formal performance appraisal system existed. (Points =1.)

9. Communication and coordination (total points = 5). The company had three totally integrated meetings involving managers from various departments: (a) the executive

committee, (b) the weekly operations meeting, and (c) the monthly information systems meeting. The executive committee did not meet regularly. Other internal meetings were a weekly human resources meeting, a merchandising meeting, and a weekly marketing meeting. (Points = 2.)

Aside from meetings concerned with day-to-day operational issues, very few project teams, task forces, or committees existed through which resources were coordinated to deal with innovations and issues of progress. (Points = 1.)

The CEO did not meet with every executive individually on a formal basis. He did, however, follow an open-door policy, and his managers could see him at short notice. He often cut through chains of authority to communicate directly with employees. The top-level team met informally on a weekly basis to talk about the various issues at hand and to discuss problems. (Points = 2.)

10. Decision-making (total points = 3). Some measure of decentralization of decision-making power occurred when four key functions were decentralized under the two regional managers; but these were subsequently centralized again. The CEO mentioned that further decentralization could still take place. (Points = 1.)

Executives and managers, particularly area managers, were not really empowered and had only a small amount of discretion in employment decisions, salary adjustments, expenditure, etc. (Points = 1.)

Functional head office departments had specific policy-making mandates within which the operating divisions had to perform. Head office management was thus prescriptive rather than consultative and supportive. A significant amount of empowerment could still occur. (Points = 1.)

11. Change and transformation (total points = 11). Few

opportunities were utilized or had been created for the CEO or other directors to sell a newly created vision to all staff. (Points = 1.)

In order to identify a need for change and redirection, market research programs were used to research and use information on trends and nuances in the external environment. (Points = 3.)

The company's new direction and strategic plan did not deviate from its previous position. Only increment changes were made. (Points = 1.)

Few structural changes took place during the review period. (Points = 1.)

Little change in products, product presentation, or market focus took place during the review period. (Points = 1.)

Except for one person, the top management team did not change at all during the review period. (Points = 1.)

The pricing structure did not change during the review period. (Points = 1.)

Few new avenues for increasing revenue were explored and implemented. (Points = 1.)

Little change in policies and values were made. (Points = 1.)

Carin ends her PowerPoint presentation and looks at her notes. "Let me summarize the intervention strategies of this declining pharmaceutical company," she says. "In-depth analysis of profit and loss accounts to determine opportunities to increase profits was made by the company. Three positions that became vacant through the course of events were not filled. To reduce costs, the finance manager, marketing director, and deputy managing director saved thousands of dollars by terminating the services of an overnight security company.

"The company made some structural changes. An administrative director was removed from the board and the credit director was forced to leave. A new operations director was appointed; he appointed a full regional team consisting of two regional managers, human resources, credit, administration, and a security manager.

"This decentralization of human resources, administration, and security did not work well; however, these functions were taken back to the head office. The human resources director was made responsible for marketing, and a new manager was appointed to assist the merchandising director.

"The commission structure was changed so that sales people would receive higher commission on higher margin products, which would facilitate the sale of more profitable products. The company introduced a "service excellence" program in which the customers evaluated the company's service. The CEO took personal responsibility for negotiations with the advertising agency and introduced a scientific staff selection program, which increased the training and development budget."

"Thank you Carin," I say.

Tim is already up and getting his presentation ready. "Tim," I say, "tell us about your declining retail company." He begins.

1. Vision and mission (total points = 6). The company had a written vision and mission statement that was also in the annual report and contained in documentation supplied to directors. (Points = 3.)

A formal process was followed in developing the mission statement during an annual three-day conference. However, this process involved only the directors of the organization and not a large group of managers. (Points = 2.)

The mission statement was not made available to the branch network. (Points = 1.)

2. Strategy and direction (total points = 6). During the review period, an annual three-day management conference was held away from the office. During this off-site conference, new priorities were set based on market research, and past successes and problems were reviewed. This led to specific actions being planned for the next year. (Points = 3.)

But this process involved only the managing director, directors, and alternate directors. The next executive level in the organization was not involved. (Points = 2.)

The results of this strategic planning process were not made available to all executives and managers, but only to directors and a few other selected executives. (Points = 1.)

3. Environmental scanning (total points = 5). In terms of specific processes through which external environmental factors could be scanned, market research was undertaken for a few years, then stopped and only resumed five years later. Branch managers and the merchandising department accumulated market statistics, but this was only done on an ad hoc basis and never developed into a continuous process, except for pricing and catalogue information, which was collected monthly. (Points = 2.)

Formal processes involving large numbers of managers were not followed. (Points = 1.)

The information from the environment was used, but its nature was usually operational rather than strategic. (Points = 2.)

4. Organizational design (total points = 4). Little change

took place in the way the organization was structured during the review period. The only change was the addition of the position of information systems manager, who reported directly to the CEO. (Points = 1.)

The head count of the company remained fairly static during the review period. (Points = 1.)

Little change took place in the composition of the top management team. The only new position was the information systems manager. (Points = 1.)

The company's structure can be classified as distinctly functional or hierarchical. There were no signs of any use of newer, more modern, structural alternatives. (Points = 1.)

5. Role definition (total points = 4). Job descriptions existed for all managers, but their content did not change during the review period. (Points = 2.)

Annual objectives were formulated as a natural result of the strategic planning process. They were developed collectively by the management team (as opposed to being prescribed by the CEO). Due to the fact that only directors were involved, the impact on the company was isolated. (Points = 2.)

6. Reward systems (total points = 4). Remuneration was based on a job-grading system, salary surveys, and contribution. (Points = 2.)

Remuneration consisted mainly of salary, the normal fringe benefits (such as health insurance, pension fund, car), and a performance bonus system based on return on gross assets. Branch managers were paid quarterly bonuses based on net profit at the branch level, regional managers on an annual basis. Up to 25 percent of annual salary could be received as a bonus. (Points = 2.)

7. Policies and values (total points = 3). A set of values was

compiled during one of the off-site management conferences, but it was not expanded on or distributed throughout the organization. No specific values program was undertaken. (Points = 1.)

The values were not marketed throughout the organization and little emphasis was placed on getting people to operate according to these values. (Points = 1.)

The company could not be described as value driven. Very little empowerment took place, and little discretion was given to managers in terms of decision-making power. (Points = 1.)

8. Performance management (total points = 4). Performance was managed over a narrow base that excluded a more comprehensive assessment of aspects, such as people development, policy and strategy development, building structures and teams, client relations, and innovation. (Points = 1.)

Activities within the organization were controlled through (a) a twice-weekly flash report covering all aspects of sales, (b) stock levels, financial charges, and debtors, (c) monthly profit and loss accounts, reports on credit statistics, and reports on merchandising statistics, (d) reports on transport and human resources, and (e) internal audits and loss control reports. This reporting system showed that financial performance was managed only through reports, with little indication of performance management happening through a network of meetings, project teams, committees, and/or other strategic processes. (Points = 2.)

No evidence was found of a formal performance appraisal system with feedback on performance. (Points = 1.)

9. Communication and coordination (total points = 4). In terms of a formal network of meetings, committees, and

project teams to facilitate communication and coordination, the following existed: (a) quarterly board meetings, (b) monthly management meetings attended by all directors and alternate directors, (c) one-on-one meetings with the CEO after each field meeting, (d) quarterly branch review meetings involving only some of the directors, and (e) an annual awards day when the managing director came into direct contact with regional managers and branch staff. Only the monthly management meetings were interdepartmental. (Points = 1.)

Communication structures in the organization were characterized as distinctly vertical rather than horizontal. No committees, project teams, or meetings were created to coordinate efforts on special issues or formulate policy. (Points = 1.)

Despite the fact that contact between the CEO and his executives was regular, it always took place on an ad hoc basis. They held no formal meetings. The CEO met formally with other staff from time to time, usually during the annual rewards day and road shows, where he and his directors went around visiting all the branches. The top executive team often met on informal occasions to discuss business. (Points = 2.)

10. Decision-making (total points = 3). The decision-making process in the organization was very centralized. Little decentralization existed. (Points = 1.)

Executives and managers were not empowered. They had little discretion or decision-making power. (Points = 1.)

Head office departments had an unhealthy degree of power in terms of prescribing to the operational network of branches how they should run their business. This was also an indication of the degree of centralized decision-making. Restrictive policies were not reduced; instead, they were

---

increased. There was no system of values to help guide the greater discretion of managers. (Points = 1.)

11. Change and transformation (total points = 11). Except for annual visits by the CEO to every branch, there were few opportunities to sell the vision and direction of the organization to employees. (Points = 1.)

In terms of market research and gathering other external information that could be used to identify the need for a change of direction, formal market research was irregularly done. (Points = 1.)

Little change in the direction of the company was initiated. The only change of direction was the establishment of another chain of stores. (Points = 1.)

There were no managerial changes to the organizational structure of the company during the review period. (Points = 1.)

Products, product presentation, and market focus did not change, except for the introduction of the new chain of stores. (Points = 2.)

The composition of the top management team remained static during this period. (Points = 1.)

The company's pricing structure did not change during the pre-turnaround phase and remained at 43 percent gross profit. (Points = 1.)

No new avenues for increasing revenue were explored or implemented. Turnover dramatically increased due to the emphasis on sales. (Points = 2.)

Policies and values systems did not change at all during the review period, except for a tightening up of policy. (Points = 1.)

"To summarize," Tim says, "we found that with the object

---

of financing a management buy-out, this declining retail company adopted a policy to push sales to achieve the greatest degree of turnover and profits and to raise funds from the banks. The credit policy was not adequately applied and with this push for sales, while volumes did increase, so did the debt. Sales budgets per branch were increased and incentives linked to these budgets to motivate sales people to sell more. More sales people were hired per branch.

"Greater emphasis was placed on outdoor sales over indoor sales. Outdoor sales are defined as when a sales representative visits customers, whereas indoor sales are when the sale takes place in the store. The ratio of outdoor to indoor sales was increased from approximately 40:60 to 80:20. Product lines per store were increased. The store network grew from 118 stores to 141 over a three-year period.

"The company was clearly positioned at the bottom end of the market. To increase sales volume, another chain of eleven stores was opened and positioned for the middle market.

"As a result of bad debts, extra credit controllers and debt collectors had to be employed. A decision was made by top management to reposition two of the three chains to represent an even spread through most economic sectors. Many of the stores changed names, brand names, and merchandise. A store belonging to one chain now belonged to another. Staff changed as well. Customers were confused and sales volume dropped.

"The credit department, which assisted branches in managing the debtors' book and had twelve field credit managers reporting directly to the credit director, was downsized to a credit director and only three others. The credit policy also changed on numerous occasions in terms of criteria for credit granting and classification of bad debt. This resulted in more confusion. Employees were paid incentives on bottom line profit in terms of cash bonuses on a quarterly basis. This resulted in a short-term focus."

Tim concludes his report and returns to his seat.

Scott is already on his feet. He opens his laptop and begins his report on his declining freight company.

1. Vision and mission (total points = 6). The mission and vision for the company were developed and updated during an annual strategic planning session, then published as part of the strategic plan. (Points = 3.)

A formal process was followed by a cross-section of managers, including the CEO, directors, and six general managers, to define the mission and the vision. (Points = 2.)

The mission and the vision appeared in the annual strategic plan and were accessible to senior management, but they were not widely communicated to other employees. (Points = 1.)

2. Strategy and direction (total points = 9). The top executive team met on an annual basis for strategic planning and to readdress the mission and the direction of the company. (Points = 3.)

This meeting normally involved the CEO, the directors, and six general managers. Time was set aside for strategic planning. The meeting was not simply an event for which time was made available in between other pressing problems. (Points = 3.)

The result of this strategic planning process was published strategic plans that led to an operations and marketing plan to be presented to the shareholders. The strategic plan was then translated into detailed budgets, which were available to all managers in the operating units. (Points = 3.)

3. Environmental scanning (total points = 6). Specific processes existed through which environmental changes were noted: (a) an outside research company performed an annual service gaps analysis, and (b) a teleservicing department, consisting of eight employees, communicated with customers on a regular basis. In addition, service quality indicators in the quality control department monitored service levels constantly. Surveys were also taken on customers' requirements. During the review period, between six and seven surveys were taken by external consultants. (Points = 3.)

While these actions took place regularly, only a small number of employees were involved. Changes in employees' attitudes were thus limited. (Points = 2.)

There was no evidence to suggest that information gained from these surveys would be used for strategic planning. The directors who were interviewed believed that survey information was not considered during strategic planning. Strategic planning also involved SWOT, the analysis of external strengths, weaknesses, opportunities, and threats. (Points = 1.)

4. Organizational design (total points = 4). The organizational structure was characterized by continuous change in the addition, subtraction, or re-emphasis of functions. Although this implied great change and would normally be a strong manifestation of the process of organizational design, most the changes had negative effects. (Points = 1.)

Major changes in the head count also took place. The company grew from 418 to 1,130 over a four-year period, and then dropped to approximately 900. It is questionable to what extent any culture can survive and maintain service levels and sound relationships with customers with such a large growth in head count. (Point = 1.)

Massive changes took place in the top management team during the period under review. The appointment of new or additional management did not seem to follow a strategic plan, but seemed to be the result of "fire-fighting." (Points = 1.)

Despite the management changes, the structure of the company did not move away from the traditional functional, hierarchical structure to accommodate newer managerial thinking or organization design. (Points = 1.)

5. Role definition (total points = 4). The roles of the company's senior executives were always clearly defined in terms of specific mandates and annual objectives and targets. (Points = 3.)

But the definitions of these roles did not flow democratically from the strategic planning. Definitions were largely prescribed by the CEO. (Points = 1.)

6. Reward systems (total points = 2). The company had a limited scope for remuneration according to contribution. (Points = 1.)

Remuneration packages consisted mainly of a cash salary, the normal fringe benefits (such as health insurance, pension fund, and company car), and a profit share of up to 25 percent of basic annual salary. But this was for executive committee members only. This super profit-sharing concept was terminated during the period under review, and thereafter no profit sharing or share participation scheme existed. (Points = 1.)

7. Policy and values (total points = 4). A set of values was developed, but it was not well documented or widely publicized in the company, nor was it used as a norm for governing behavior.

Values were determined during the strategic planning meeting, but were not incorporated into a specific program to bring about a cultural shift. (Points = 2.)

In the organizational culture, everything was counted, reported on, and measured through endless reports and statistics. In this way, the culture tended to be autocratic. Because the company was largely policy and measurement driven, it achieved little by way of empowering managers or granting them any discretion in decision-making regarding employment, strategy, and structure. (Points = 1.)

No evidence existed that the values of the company were advocated as a norm according to which behavior could be governed. (Points = 1.)

8. Performance management (total points = 3). The company's activities were mainly controlled through the monthly financial results and other statistically-oriented reports. Most of the controlling took place during the monthly executive committee meeting. (Points = 1.)

Performance during the review period was primarily managed around financial issues. There was no comprehensive assessment on the basis of aspects such as people development, building structures and teams, client relations, and innovation. (Points = 1.)

No formal performance management system existed. (Points = 1.)

9. Communication and coordination (total points = 5). There were some interdepartmental and interdisciplinary meetings, project teams, and committees that facilitated coordination and communication. The executive committee met on a monthly basis, and there was a board meeting every quarter. Apart from these two meetings, which looked at

the business from a strategic point of view and cut across divisional boundaries, however, the only other meetings were departmental meetings and a few project teams that investigated issues like pricing, cost per parcel, and proof of delivery. (Points = 2.)

Little evidence existed of true horizontal communications. We gained the impression that communication was largely hierarchical and vertical, down the chain of command within departments and divisions, rather than across departments and divisions. Some committees and project teams were created to coordinate efforts on special issues or to formulate policy. (Points = 2.)

The CEO did not formally meet with executives on a weekly basis. There were very few opportunities where he met with employees other than with his direct reportees, and he seldom received those staff members in his office. The top management team often met on an informal basis to discuss business. (Points = 1.)

10. Decision-making (total points = 3). No decentralization of decision-making power took place during the period under review. The company was largely run on a centralized basis. (Points = 1.)

Executives and managers were never really empowered. They had little discretion in decisions concerning employment of staff, termination of services, salary adjustments, expenditure, and/or credit grading. (Points = 1.)

Management actions revealed strong centralized control, prescription, and dictation to operations staff. There was no clear evidence that current policies had been changed to make way for a value-driven culture or impart greater discretion to managers. (Point = 1.)

11. Change and transformation (total points = 10). Apart from the annual strategic planning session, few opportunities were created to sell the strategic direction of the company. (Points = 1.)

Although market research was carried out and other external sources of information existed, these were largely ignored and not used to support the strategic direction of the company. (Points = 1.)

The direction of the company emerging at the time of the study did not deviate much, if at all, from the strategy of three years before. Hardly any adjustments had been made to cope with the increasing customer dissatisfaction. (Points = 1.)

During the three years, the structure of the company changed, but far too much and without apparent plan. This necessitated a negative evaluation. (Points = 1.)

During the period under review, neither product nor product presentation nor market focus changed from the initial strategic choice. The company was unable to cope with the impending crisis. (Points = 1.)

The top management team changed to such an extent and with such apparent lack of strategy that it dictated a negative evaluation. (Points = 1.)

Although the pricing structure was changed in line with the company's new direction, it was rigidly implemented and enforced despite forces in the environment indicating the need for change. (Points = 1.)

During the period under review, some new avenues for increasing revenue were explored and implemented. (Points = 2.)

Corporate policies and values did not change during the review period. (Points = 1.)

"If we summarize the intervention strategies of this declining freight company," Scott says, "we find the following. The company continued with a strategy of massive growth and expansion. After the previous CEO and a director visited Federal Express in the USA, the company implemented an extremely high-tech operating system that included the use of hand-held computers to capture data on the jobs of delivery drivers. The company also created a new position of assistant courier to assist couriers and drivers in this new function.

"The company closed down 110 agencies across the country that had been managed by entrepreneurial franchisees. It opened regional offices to support deliveries to smaller towns that had no freight service. When the company dismissed the operations director who objected to this system, this actually increased delivery time per parcel.

"A new financial director and 185 additional employees were hired, some to assist the courier in his new duties, others to help sort out problems in the POS system. The company introduced a new training program to increase customer service and product knowledge. The company believed it needed more competent staff. It attracted more qualified people through increased salaries and fringe benefits, but in the process upset so many existing staff members that this led to 38 percent turnover for that year.

"A new super-plant was commissioned. When the company merged with a smaller similar company, employees were told they were going to be laid off. Although a layoff never happened, this fact was never communicated to them and morale suffered.

"When the company made a strategic decision to focus on the customer market for greater sales volumes rather than on the blue-chip corporate logistics market, conflict arose between the marketing director and the operations director. The marketing director did not believe this strategy would work. This conflict resulted in the operations director hiring his own sales team of fifty representatives to capture the consumer market. Based on an organization and methods study indicating that the consumer market was more profitable, the pricing structure was changed to maximize margins. The marketing division did research and found that the customer wanted to pay per consignment, rather than per parcel, as the new pricing policy dictated. These research findings were not heeded.

"The general manager of operations eliminated a complete layer of regional managers. A new general manager of domestic operations was hired and within six months the layer of regional managers was reintroduced. The new hires came from outside the company. Within a year, the general manager of operations was asked to leave the company.

The company re-engineered the entire computer-driven operation system to coincide with and facilitate the merger mentioned above. Only three months were allowed to do this re-engineering; $3 million later, the system collapsed and the architect of the system resigned with all re-engineering plans undocumented.

"The company restructured the branch network and changed the status of the branches from profit centers to merely cost centers. They were only to handle parcels at a given cost, and all their other functions – sales, marketing, servicing, accounting, and credit control and billing – were removed from the branches and centralized. The head count grew by 350 people to 1,350." At this point, his presentation finished, Scott closes his laptop and takes his seat.

For the first time since the start of our mission to discover the strategies and competencies of successful corporate turnaround or recovery executives, I now fully realize how much work my team has put into this project. I know that I must remember to formally thank them when this is over.

We end the day with plans to discuss each of the eleven organizational processes as they were manifested across the eight companies tomorrow morning.

chapter 14

FRIDAY MORNING ARRIVES, and everyone is looking forward to the weekend. "Today," I say as I call the team to order, "we will discuss each of the eleven organizational processes as they were manifested across the companies you researched." I open my PowerPoint presentation. "I spent just about all of last night putting together some notes from our discussions for today." I click and the slides begin.

1. Mission and vision. Companies that recovered successfully differed significantly from companies in financial decline in the process of formulating vision and mission.

"Companies that were recovered and financially successful," I say, reading from my notes, "had a clearly defined mission. They followed a distinct process to develop this mission, and a large cross-section of managers was involved. The mission appeared frequently in company documentation and was accessible to all employees.

"Companies in decline, on the other hand, had a mission statement only occasionally. The CEO and some directors, but not middle management, developed it. It seldom appeared in company literature and was not accessible to all employees."

2. Strategy and direction. The recovered and declining companies did not differ significantly.

"Companies that were successfully recovered," I say, "were no more likely than the declining companies to follow a formal strategic planning process or to involve more managers than the CEO alone or with directors or general managers.

"What we found was that in the recovery of a group, strategic planning can play a significant role."

3. Environmental scanning. The process of environmental scanning differed in recovered and declining companies. Significant differences existed regarding issues of external focus, environmental scanning, and the importation of new information into the organization for strategic and decision-making processes.

"Financially successful companies that had been turned around and recovered from low financial performance tended to use more external sources of information, more frequently and habitually, instead of on an ad hoc basis. Furthermore, recovered companies tended to involve more of their managers in this environmental scanning for real organizational change and refocusing of their business.

"Declining companies, on the other hand, were more likely to be internally focused. They did not research external information, and where they did find it, using it did not become a habitual process. Information gathered was not used to its fullest extent to change attitude, culture, or business.

"Groups of companies held the top positions on the raw score distribution. This tells us that groups of companies were far more externally focused than operating companies.

"In terms of manufacturing and non-manufacturing companies," I conclude, "no significant differences existed."

4. Organizational design. Successfully recovered companies were more likely than declining companies to have made major changes to their structure.

"Significant reductions in head count took place," I say, "as well as major changes to the composition of their executive teams. They also made greater use of modern design principles than declining companies.

"Declining companies were characterized by little change to their structures, marginal reduction in head count, less change in the composition of their executive teams, and less use of modern design principles. The manufacturing and group organizations both had high scores, which may indicate that manufacturing concerns and group companies were open to organization design as an intervention strategy to increase productivity and profitability.

"Another way of looking at this is that the top scoring companies, all of which were recovered companies, belong to either manufacturing or group organizations."

5. Role definition. Financially successfully companies differed significantly from declining companies on the issue of role definition and clarification.

I read from my notes again. "We found that the recovered companies were generally more likely than declining companies to have job descriptions and sets of objectives to guide the actions and behavior of their executives and managers.

"These job descriptions and objectives were also more likely to flow logically from the strategic planning process, and each executive job definition and set of objectives tended to form a synergy supporting the overall corporate direction.

"Declining companies, on the other hand, were less likely to have job descriptions or specific objectives for executives. When objectives were set, few processes existed to integrate them with overall corporate objectives or other division and department objectives. No differentiation existed between manufacturing and non-manufacturing companies regarding this process."

6. Reward systems. A significant difference existed between recovered companies and declining companies.

Again, I read from my notes. "Recovered and financially successful companies were more likely to base remuneration on a broader base than job grading and salary scales. Remuneration also included contribution and, in some cases, non-financial performance, such as innovation, creativity, people development, and so forth. The nature of these companies' reward structures was also flexible, with a high level of profit sharing, share participation, and flexible, cafeteria-type reward systems.

"Declining companies, in contrast, based their remuneration mostly on job grading and salary surveys. Only in exceptional cases would contribution be a criterion and hardly ever non-financial indices, such as product development, innovation, and leadership. Reward structures of declining companies tended to comprise salary and normal standard range of fringe benefits; they seldom included profit sharing, share participating, or flexible reward systems.

"Most of the group companies that had been recovered were at the top of this section. It could be argued that group companies were more likely to manifest stronger processes regarding rewards and remuneration.

7. Values and policies. Successfully recovered companies that were financially successful usually had a set of values created in an organizational development program. These sets of values were available to all employees.

"These organizations also moved toward a value-driven culture than declining companies. Most of the recovering companies achieved high raw scores, which indicate a strong process to establish a value-driven culture.

"Declining companies were less likely to have followed a process to develop values. Employees were not involved in formulating a set of values. These organizations were largely driven by their policies and procedures manuals."

8. Performance management. Financially successful companies that had been recovered were more

likely to base their performance measurement on factors beyond financial indices, such as people development, team building, and innovation.

I turn a page in my notes. "Performance was managed not only through the financial month-end results but also through various project teams and committees. Successful companies were likely to have a formal performance management system in place for each executive, a system extending beyond simple performance appraisals to include elements of career management.

"Declining companies tended to base performance measurement only on financial criteria and to manage it only through the monthly financial results. They were less likely to have formal performance management systems in place.

9. Communication and coordination. Financially successful companies were more likely than declining companies to be managed through interdepartmental meetings and committees that facilitate coordination.

"Successful companies tended to be characterized by a network structure of interdisciplinary task forces and committees that regulated matters of mutual interest. The CEOs of these companies were more likely to have more contact with employees beyond their direct reportees.

"Declining companies were less likely to have interdepartmental meetings and less likely to have a network structure of interdisciplinary task forces and committees. They tended to be more segmentalist than integrative. Communication was more vertical than horizontal. Non-manufacturing companies seemed to have a stronger tendency for managing through network structures than manufacturing companies. The group companies had a high raw score, which indicates that the group companies may have a stronger process governing communication and coordination than operating companies."

10. Decision making. Successfully recovered companies tended to have more decentralized decision making that gave executives and managers more discretion in decisions such as appointment of additional staff, salary increases, leases, credit terms, and so forth. They also had less prescription from central head office departments to operations.

"Declining companies, in contrast, tended to be more centralized. They permitted less discretion and had a strong central head office department dictating policies within which the operational side of the business had to function.

"The group companies again had a high score, which leads us to conclude that group companies tended to be more decentralized in their decision-making than operating companies. The manufacturing concerns were fairly evenly spread across the rankings, and no differences seemed to exist between manufacturing and service companies on decision-making powers."

11. Change and transformation. The management teams of successfully recovered companies initiated far more change and transformation than the declining companies regarding the following.

Another slide glides into view.

1. The company's vision
2. Use of external information
3. Direction of the company
4. Structure
5. Product and product presentation
6. Membership of the top executive team
7. Pricing policies
8. Exploring sources of revenue
9. Values and policies.

"Declining companies," I say after the team has noted these nine points, "were characterized by less manifestation of change in these areas. They were less inclined, or more reluctant, to bring about real change in their organizations regarding the items listed.

"Group companies did not dominate the highest rankings here as they did in some of the previously discussed items, although they were all above the median.

"All of the recovered manufacturing companies were above the median. We can conclude that change and transformation seems more critical in manufacturing than in service industries.

"In conclusion," I say, looking around the table at my team, "these findings seem to offer some insight into the relationship between key organizational processes and the financial performance of a business. In addition, they give an indication of how some successfully recovered businesses went about structuring key organizational processes and, further, how the neglect of organizational process can, in the case of the declining business, result in an apparent inability to reverse their fortunes."

"Excuse me," Tim says, looking at his watch and standing up. "There's something I need to take care of in the office." With that he disappears through the door.

"How about a lunch break?" offers Scott. We all nod, as John says, "Good idea."

✳ ✳ ✳

At 2 p.m. we are all seated again in mission control. John is ready to discuss the findings on the competencies and personalities of the CEOs whose companies have been recovered. He turns our attention to his PowerPoint presentation and begins.

1. Managerial competence. The results obtained from the managerial assessment were the findings of the four CEOs of successfully recovered organizations as compared to the assessment results of a control group of CEOs.

The CEOs were all male. The average age of the CEOs of recovered companies was 47, with a range from 41 to 56; the average age of the CEOs in the control group was 46, with a range from 39 to 56. The investigation group had an average of 6.5 years of college education, whereas the control group had an average of 4.3 years

For the purpose of these comparisons, a directional hypothesis was formulated: the CEOs of recovered companies would outscore the control group. A test of significance was given to all CEOs in both groups being studied.

The CEOs of successfully recovered businesses demonstrated a much stronger behavioral manifestation and competence in handling the managerial situations described below.

a. Problem solving. The CEOs of successfully recovered organizations showed a significantly stronger ability to think conceptually about a problem than the control group. They showed a significantly greater intelligence and creativity to formulate questions and gather information about the problem. They demonstrated a stronger ability to integrate information and formulate conclusions and reason. They further demonstrated a superior ability to anticipate what action would solve the problem at hand.

b. General management. The CEOs of the successfully recovered companies exhibited a significantly stronger ability to handle general management situations than the control group.

The CEOs of recovered companies initiated more action than the control group in a given time period and acted with greater innovation and more proactively.

The CEOs of recovered companies were significantly stronger in their ability and competence to understand the complexities of the issues they had to deal with and to see the implications that a particular issue might have for other issues and their interrelationships and effects on each other.

In terms of consequences, the CEOs of recovered companies demonstrated an ability to initiate action and propose solutions that would have further-reaching, positive consequences than the control group. In that their actions and solutions are more clearly and more closely aligned with the requirements of the situation, they generally exhibited better judgment than the control group.

The CEOs of recovered companies had a clearer perception, i.e., a better reading, of management situations. Their responses to these situations were more appropriate to the requirements of the situation than the control group.

The CEOs of recovered companies were more inclined to use people effectively through delegation, decentralization, and empowerment. The control group CEOs also delegated well, but tended to reserve final decision making once the person they had delegated had done the investigation and feasibility studies. The CEOs of recovered companies not only asked people to analyze and investigate and bring their recommendations to them for approval, but they also empowered people by making them responsible for the total process, from fact-finding to analysis and formulation of a solution, up to and including decision-making within given parameters. Furthermore, the CEOs of recovered companies were better able to make sound arrangements in terms of the planning and organizing needed to handle these management situations.

The CEOs of recovered companies were not, however, significantly more decisive than the control group and therefore did not show a stronger tendency to act decisively or make quick decisions.

The CEOs of recovered companies demonstrated a competence in general management superior to 94 percent of the managers in the data bank, whereas the control group CEOs did better than 75 percent.

    c. Staff management. The CEOs of recovered

companies exhibited strong competencies in staff management.

d. Output of work. A significant difference was noted between the two groups in terms of their output of work. This difference in the averages of the two groups indicates that the CEOs of recovered companies have a greater capacity for achievement. They could handle more work and deal with more issues in a given time than the control group CEOs.

e. Overall profile. The CEOs of recovered companies demonstrated a significantly better ability across all behavioral competencies than the control group.

f. Cognitive capacity. Probably the most significant difference between the CEOs of recovered companies and the control group lies in their levels of cognitive capacity and levels of strategic and abstract thinking.

CEOs of recovered companies possessed a significantly stronger cognitive capacity to think:

- Holistically rather than segmentally
- Futuristically rather than historically
- Conceptually rather than pedantically
- In terms of process rather than events/incidents.

CEOs of recovered companies also tended to function at a higher level of cognitive capacity than the control group. They seemed to deal more in concepts and universals, whereas the control group dealt to a greater extent in symbols.

2. Personality. The CEOs of successfully recovered

companies differed significantly from the control group in the following factors:

a. Initiating. This factor consists of the need to control and influence others and have a preference for initiating a style of leadership.

Control group CEOs demonstrated a stronger initiating style than the CEOs of recovered companies. They exhibited a significantly stronger need to influence and control others, and to shape and change situations. The control group CEOs were progressive and quick off the mark, initiating action and indicating direction in a more decisive manner than the CEOs of recovered companies. They tended to be impatient, to press harder for action and progress, and were likely to be autocratic and confrontational.

The CEOs of recovered companies also had a need to be in control and to take charge of people and events. They wanted to know what was going on in their business and wanted to influence others and shape and change the direction of their organizations. The control group, however, demonstrated these needs more strongly.

The implication of this finding for corporate recovery may be that as a result of their lower need for initiating behavior, the CEOs of recovered companies may create a climate where the managers in their teams receive sufficient direction, but not so much that they feel disempowered. The control group CEOs may need to influence to such an extent that their managers feel stifled in terms of how much they can initiate, innovate, and give individual recognition to what they do.

The CEOs of recovered companies seemed to maintain a good balance between their own need for intervention and degree of latitude and empowerment they give their management teams.

b.   Challenging. Here was another difference between the two groups. The construct of challenging consists of the need for challenge, a preference for the role of operator, and a belief in resolving conflict with others.

Control group CEOs were more open than the CEOs of recovered companies to accept new challenges, as presented in taking on more responsibilities, putting themselves under pressure, and generally setting high demands for themselves.

Control group CEOs believed that differences between people have to be resolved. They exhibited little tolerance for disagreement. Their style with team members was even somewhat adversarial, rather than cooperative. In people issues, they believed in the resolution of conflict and would not avoid differences.

The implications of this for corporate recovery are interesting. A co-producer of successful recovery might be the fact that the CEOs of recovered companies were less challenging and thus more contemplative in their approach. Their lower need for initiating and challenging might lead to an atmosphere and culture that is less adversarial, less directional, and less controlling. This can result in people having more space for their own ideas and opinions. Such a culture would lead to the creation and stimulation of intrapreneurs who feel that they have room to move and to use their initiative in solving their own and the organization's problems.

---

c. Integrating. There was no significant difference between the two groups. This factor consists of a preference for an integrative style, a need for affiliation, a need for social extension, a belief in network communication, and a belief in participative decision making.

d. Goal direction. The construct of goal direction consists of the need to set and meet goals, the need for assertion and/or dominance, and the need for composure.

The CEOs of recovered companies demonstrated a significantly stronger need to set objectives and work according to objectives. They were also more persistent in pursuing what they set out to achieve. They did not like to deviate from their plans and strategies.

Regarding a need for composure, the CEOs of recovered companies liked to feel that they were emotionally in control of situations. They were more inclined to remain calm, collected, and composed under emotionally stressful situations, such as rejection and criticism from others. They were less inclined to feel threatened or to lose their tempers. Control group CEOs tended to be more "touchy" and could be more inclined to lose their tempers under stress. They may have felt more threatened and insecure than the CEOs of recovered companies.

The implication of this for corporate recovery is that the new CEO appointed to recover an ailing business in financial crisis enters a volatile situation. The need to pursue a recovery strategy with confidence, conviction, and assertion and to handle criticism from various stakeholders is essential.

Relentless pursuit of the essential objectives is required.

e. Problem-solving. No significant difference was found between the two groups in terms of their preference for problem-solving behavior. They were about equal in terms of their need for change, their propensity to search for information and ideas from others and their external environment, and in choosing either traditional or radical work methods.

Both groups had stronger needs for problem-solving behaviors, such as researching, change, and unconventional methods, than most managers in the data bank. They exhibited dissatisfaction with the status quo and strove to find unique solutions to problems.

f. Implementing. There seem to be no differences between the two groups in the personality construct of implementing. CEOs in both groups were less inclined than most other managers in the data bank to prefer the managerial role of completer. They had a lower need for structure. This indicates that both groups of CEOs were disinclined to be systematic and structured or to get too involved in detail. Both groups could function well in an ambiguous, under-structured environment.

John shuts off his PowerPoint and nods to the group.

"Thank you, John," I say. I address the entire team now.

"As we discuss the findings we found in summary, that CEOs of recovered companies, when compared with

CEOs in the control group, seemed to show a greater competence in solving problems and making decisions (fact finding, anticipation, and reasoning power) and handling general management situations (initiative, understanding, consequences, arrangements, decisiveness, and delegation).

"The CEOs of recovered companies showed a greater cognitive capacity and facility for holistic, strategic thinking. They possessed a greater facility in terms of the volume of work they could handle. They were also more concerned with being goal directed and less concerned with initiating or challenging.

"These CEOs were more competent at problem-solving and decision-making, and thus analytical and decision-making skills were important in the turnaround situation.

"These CEOs have a stronger ability to delegate. They also have a preference for implementing, motivating, and achieving results through others. The characteristics of being action-oriented and enthusiastic, plus significantly higher levels of action initiated and output during the general management situation, are also attributes of the successful recovery executive."

I end there and add, "Thank you, team. Seeing that it's Friday, and only 4 o'clock, let's get an early start to our weekend. On Monday, we will conclude our examination of our research findings."

chapter 15

IT'S MONDAY MORNING, and the commute seems longer than usual. I think this is because today is the last day of our reporting after almost a year of research and work on this project. I am excited that my team has worked so well. What they have accomplished is phenomenal.

Arriving at the office, I park my BMW in my assigned parking space as I have done for the last ten years. I walk in the front door as usual, but instead of my usual automatic greeting to Linda, I stop and ask her, "How are you this morning, Linda?" I don't think I've ever done this before, and it takes Linda by surprise.

"Err...f–fine, thank you, Adam," she stammers. "How about you?"

"Well, Linda, this is the best day of my life!" And with that I saunter into my office to take off my coat and put my briefcase down.

As I walk into mission control, all four team members are present and ready to conclude the project. After I greet them, I am ready to switch on my laptop.

Our research indicates that a relationship did exist between the successful recovery of a business organization from declining or inadequate economic and financial performance, and the following:

- The managerial competence, cognitive capacity, and personality factors of the CEO
- The management actions or major initiatives taken and intervention strategies chosen to direct the activities of the organization
- The nature and structure of key managerial and organizational processes that guide the behavior of the organization.

These findings have, to a varying degree, shed light on the following:

- The personality constructs, preferred managerial styles, and values of the executive of a successfully recovered company
- The behavior patterns and thought processes of the successful executive
- The major initiatives or intervention strategies used to recover an ailing business organization
- How key management and organizational processes are structured to co-produce the recovery.

These findings hold important implications for a number of key issues in management. It is our finding that the major research studies on corporate turnaround indicate the universality of recovery strategies. All organizations – small or large, consumer or capital/product, first world or third world, private or public, high-tech or low-tech, young or mature, deeply sick or marginally sick – *all* of these exhibit common elements in the co-producers of their declines and the strategies used to recover them.

And it's not only business corporations that go into decline and are regenerated. So do other collectivities, such as non-profit organizations, communities, and whole societies. Non-business organizations can also recover and regenerate themselves, and they seem to use very similar processes. Our research supports the findings that a great similarity exists in the recovered companies regarding the success of certain strategies, regardless of variables such as size, duration of crisis, or nature of industry. These similarities are distinct and quite different from the similarities found in declining companies. It is also interesting to note that universal intervention strategies also apply equally to business organizations in different social systems.

We found that when influential writers in the field look at *strategic management*, they sometimes overemphasized seeking niches in the market, portfolio management, and other market-oriented and externally focused actions. Because of this, they neglected the people management and process management issues as powerful strategic options.

Influential literature on corporate turnaround and recovery showed the limitations of strategy. Some writers found a negative correlation between strategic elements of recovery, such as diversification, product line rationalization, expansion, etc., and rate of gain in profitability. During turnaround, "strategic gaming" does not work and in fact decelerates the turnaround effort.

Relatively little time and effort were spent on product-market focusing as an intervention strategy in recovery. Far more emphasis was put on internal factors, such as developing the organization, establishing a philosophy and culture, integrating organization design, and building the executive team.

The *biological metaphor*, which has been influencing organizational theory, draws a parallel between organizations and living beings in their birth, development, maturation, and crisis. This is where the parallel ends, however, because while all living beings must die, organizations need not and do not die. That's why organizational death is a remote occurrence. Organizations that do go into liquidation are usually small, marginal companies, but seldom do we see the demise of sizeable, complex organizations. They change ownership or identity, they grow, they decline, they merge and acquire or are acquired, they undergo strategic and structural metamorphoses, but they seldom die or cease to operate altogether.

The reason why collectivities such as business organizations seldom die is twofold. First, their built-in inefficiency of multiple decision-makers, problem-solvers, information processors, machines, sites, and sources of finance – things that make a business more complex and slow down its operation – also guarantees that the organization will survive beyond the death of its individual members. Second the state of diverse constituencies guarantees survival because all of these constituencies have a vested interest in the continuation of the organization.

However, while the structural complexity of the collectivity and the diversity of its stakeholders guarantee its survival and continuation from generation to generation, these are ironically also the reason for its decline. The conflicting interests of diverse stakeholders can also result in an organization becoming immobilized in a crisis of directional push and pull.

When we look at *crisis and change management*, we see that there exist in an organization the seeds for destruction that, given the correct environment, will lead to distinct reasons for decline. CEOs fail to see the changes in their growth cycle and do not respond to internal turmoil created by changed external factors, which can be of a social, economical, or legal nature. This crisis period in an organization's life is generally referred to as a *corporate turnaround or recovery situation*. Recovery actions must be implemented. The terms *corporate regeneration* and *reconstruction* are also used.

Business managers are usually very literate in financial terms because financial issues can be reduced to finite exactness. Non-financial issues are, however, more difficult to understand, as they are subjective and do not lend themselves to quantification. Financial crises are thus often the result of an executive's inability to cope with the human and organizational problems he must also face.

The results of our findings shed light on these phases of decline and recovery. They also enhance our understanding of these human and organizational issues in terms of how some organizations went about making changes. Intervention strategies and phases of corporate recovery, as they emerged through the literature study and this research, further add to our knowledge of how to change and transform a business organization.

The characteristics and competencies of the turnaround executive have implications for leadership development. A strong indication emerged from our research as to what competencies need to be developed and acquired to successfully manage the processes and strategies needed to recover a business. These competencies can obviously be used to guide the selection of CEOs to manage ailing companies or those with lackluster performance. They can also be used to identify potential up and coming young managers to be groomed as corporate lifesavers.

"This," I say, looking around the table, "is where we, as a consulting firm, can add some extra value to our present and prospective customers.

"Looking at the interpretation of the results of your research, I realize that it has been interpreted by your frame of reference and contextual understanding, but you are fully aware of the fact that others could and would attach alternative or supportive interpretations to the same findings.

"When I look at the reliability of your findings, I see an issue of great importance: *quantitative research.* In the context of qualitative research, with what you have done, all meaning is 'indexical,' in that it will change as the occasion changes and as it is used in different ways. The solution to this 'indexicality' is to 'theorise' your findings or observations by identifying the patterns of influence on the research setting and developing an account of how they played their part in the outcome of the study.

"When I look at validity, this is often referred to as the extent to which the constructs measured can be correlated with other measures of the same construct. In this regard, *quantitative* research differs markedly from *qualitative* research. Quantitative research aims in its design to control and eliminate as many variables as possible that may contaminate the observation of the phenomenon the researcher wishes to study. In qualitative research, 'ecological' validity is actually enhanced when the phenomenon under study is observed in its natural setting with as many variables exercising its influence on it as are normally the case.

"This has an impact on the correctness of interpretation of the results and on their predictive validity. The way around this limitation is for the research project to be described in sufficient detail so as to enable us to evaluate the phenomena you uncovered in your research, particularly their relationships with other variables that may have influenced your observations.

"In the assessment of *managerial competencies, cognitive capacity,* and *personality and managerial styles* of the CEOs studied, the assessment instruments were of our choice. Another researcher might have chosen different techniques.

"In the *classification of intervention strategies,* each initiative was counted as one point for the purpose of the calculation of the proportions of intervention classes that contributed to recovery. However, the impact or influence of actions can differ, and no attempt was made to use a scoring system that can differentiate in terms of the degree of influence of each action. Actions were simply counted as equally significant. The purpose was to simplify classification and scoring and eliminate unnecessary subjective evaluation of the extent of an action's impact.

"When you interviewed CEOs who had successfully recovered the organizations they were managing, you asked them to cite all actions taken during the recovery and to describe the management processes in their organizations. They were aware of the fact that you, the researcher, were doing the research for the purpose of helping other companies in the same situation. It was on this basis that their participation was secured.

"We researchers therefore assumed that our respondents were motivated to recount a success story and that their discourse of the events leading to the recovery was a reflection of their understanding of how to turn around a business in crisis. Each interview was a distillation of the key issues the CEOs believed were important to the recovery. When they cited an action as important, this might have told us more about a CEO'S philosophy than about the quality of its implementation. Therefore, we may conclude that an action taken is as much a reading of what the CEO believed in as a list of actions actually carried out.

"This was similar in the case of the declining organizations where there were directors involved. They were probably inclined to cite their honest attempts to turn their companies around, therefore also expressing their belief about what is important to do in such a crisis."

I turn off my laptop and conclude. "Thank you, team, for your hard work and determination."

We all embrace. The work of our team in this mission to find another way to add value to our company and by adding another product line for our present and future customers is significant. We have found that certain elements of a corporate recovery strategy were more successful than others, that successfully recovered organizations structured key organizational processes differently, and that the CEOs of recovered organizations possess distinct personality characteristics, behavioral competencies, and cognitive capacities. We have achieved **MISSION POSSIBLE**.

appendix

1. Baden-Fuller, C., & Stopford, J.M. (1994): *Rejuvenating the mature business.* MA: Harvard Business School Press.

Bibeault, D.B. (1982): *Corporate turnaround: How managers turn losers into winners.* New York: McGraw-Hill.

Hedge, M.C. (1982): *Western and Indian models of turnaround management.* Vikalpha, 7, 289-304.

Hofer, C.W. (summer, 1980)" *Turnaround strategies.* Journal of Business Strategy, 1, 19-31.

O'Neill, H.M. (March, 1986): *An analysis of the turnaround strategy in commercial banking.* Journal of Management Studies, 23. P 165-188.

O'Shaughnessy, N.J. (1986): *Tactics for turnaround.* Management Decision, 24, 3-6.

Potts, M., & Behr, P. (1987): *The leading edge: CEOs who turned their companies around-what they did and how they did it.* New Delhi: Tata McGraw-Hill.

Schendel,D., D.Patton, G.R., Riggs, T. (1976): *Corporate turnaround strategies: A study of profit decline and recovery.* Journal of General Management, 3, 3-12.

Stuart, V., & Chadwick, V. (1987): *Changing trains: Messages for management from the Scottish Rail challenge.* Newton Abbot: David & Charles.

Smart, C., & Vertinsky, I. (July-September, 1984): *Strategy and the environment-a study of corporate responses to crisis.* Strategic Management Journal, 5, 199-213.

Slatter, S. (1984): *Corporate recovery: A guide to turnaround management.* Harmondsworth. Penquin Books.

2. Khandwalla, P.N. (1992): *Innovative corporate turnarounds.* London. Sage Publications.

3. Baden-Fuller, C., & Stopford, J.M. (1994): *Rejuvenating the mature business.* MA: Harvard Business School Press.

4. Hambrick, D.C., & Schecter, S.M. (1983): *Turnaround strategies for mature industrial-product business units.* Academy of Management Journal, 26, 231-248.

5. Baden-Fuller, C., & Stopford, J.M. (1994): *Rejuvenating the mature business.* MA: Harvard Business School Press.

Hofer, C.W. (summer, 1980): *Turnaround strategies.* Journal of Business Strategy, 1, 19-31.

Khandwalla, P.N. (1992): *Innovative corporate turnarounds.* London. Sage Publications.

O'Neill, H.M. (March, 1986): *An analysis of the turnaround strategy in commercial banking.* Journal of Management Studies, 23. 165-188.

Schendel,D., D.Patton, G.R., Riggs, T. (1976): *Corporate turnaround strategies: A study of profit decline and recovery.* Journal of General Management, 3, 3-12.

Slatter, S. (1984): *Corporate recovery: A guide to turnaround management.* Harmondsworth. Penquin Books.

6. Slatter, S. (1984): *Corporate recovery: A guide to turnaround management.* Harmondsworth. Penquin Books.

7. Gopinath, C. (1991): *Turnaround: Recognising decline and initiating intervention.* Long Range Planning, 24, 96-101.

8. Gopinath, C. (1991): *Turnaround: Recognising decline and initiating intervention.* Long Range Planning, 24, 96-101.

9. Khandwalla, P.N. (1992): *Innovative corporate turnarounds.* London. Sage Publications.

10. Gopinath, C. (1991): *Turnaround: Recognising decline and initiating intervention.* Long Range Planning, 24, 96-101.

11. Baden-Fuller, C., & Stopford, J.M. (1994): *Rejuvenating the mature business.* MA: Harvard Business School Press.

Bibeault, D.B. (1982): *Corporate turnaround: How managers turn losers into winners.* New York: McGraw-Hill.

Slatter, S. (1984): *Corporate recovery: A guide to turnaround management.* Harmondsworth. Penquin Books.

Nelson, R., & Clutterbuck, D. (1988): *Turnaround: How twenty well-known companies came back from the brink.* London: Mercury Books.

12. O'Neill, H.M. (March, 1986): *An analysis of the turnaround strategy in commercial banking.* Journal of Management Studies, 23. P 165-188.

13. Winn, J. (1993): *Performance measure for corporate decline and turnaround.* Journal of General Management, 19. P 48-63.

14. Khandwalla, P.N. (1992): *Innovative corporate turnarounds.* London. Sage Publications.

15. Mintzberg, H., Raisinghani, D., & Theoret, A. (1976): *The structure of unstructured decision-processes.* Administrative Science Quarterly, 21. P 246-275.

16. Winn, J. (1993): *Performance measure for corporate decline and turnaround.* Journal of General Management, 19. P 48-63.

17. Khandwalla, P.N. (1992): *Innovative corporate turnarounds*. London. Sage Publications.

18. Jaques, E., & Clement, S.D. (1994): *Executive leadership: A practical guide to managing complexity*. Arlington: Cason Hall.

19. Khandwalla, P.N. (1992): *Innovative corporate turnarounds*. London. Sage Publications.

www.ingramcontent.com/pod-product-compliance
Lightning Source LLC
Chambersburg PA
CBHW031835170526
45157CB00001B/304